Why should I be good? Salvation is free!

RICHARD LEE SPINOS

DEDICATION

To Sandra my amazing wife and lifetime partner who has both challenged and encouraged me as a man, husband, father and pastor, and has inspired our sons to be the men of God that have made childbearing a joy for both of us.

To all those servants of God who sometimes struggle with the thought that their labor of love may go unnoticed . . .

. . . and to all those who never stopped to think about the tragedy of a wasted stewardship that will go up in flames because what should have been edified with gold, silver and precious stones, was built with wood, hay and stubble. (1Corinthians 3:12)

WHY SHOULD I BE GOOD? SALVATION IS FREE!

PREFACE

The idea for this book started as a Facebook page of articles and dialogs concerning the salvation by works vs. grace debate. Comments, arguments and criticism began to appear on the page and I began to interact with people from all sides of the debate. I began to grow in my suspicion that many Christians today and possibly the great majority of them do not fully understand the nature of grace and the part it plays in salvation without mixing it with sanctification. I hope to show that Scripture treats salvation and sanctification as completely separate and distinct operations of God in the life of His people.

The two main lines of thinking regarding the works vs. grace debate are Arminianism and Calvinism. Being theological terms many Christians today would not be able to identify which position has influenced their thinking concerning salvation and sanctification.

Those Christians who tend towards the Calvinistic position generally have a good grasp of the nature of grace and the role it plays in salvation but tragically, in many cases, end up being nominal Christians and don't see much of a need for practical holiness or at least fail to see a sufficient lack of it in their own lives.

Christians who tend towards the Armenian position see the dire need for practical holiness. As a result, they strive to be pure and holy and are often better behaved and disciplined than their Calvinistic counterparts. However, many of these Christians struggle with the application of the principle of grace. They often feel frustrated by the experience of alternating self-condemnation and self-justification and tend to be more judgmental of others.

There are positive characteristics pertaining to each position but there are also negative consequences in adhering to one position or the other. This is exactly the difficulty. The great controversy lies in the pursuit of a harmonious synthesis of these two seemingly contradictory positive principles: grace and works; dependence on God and dependence on human effort; resting in God and laboring in His will.

This book is an attempt to present a paradigm that stresses the dire need of God's people to consider the eternal plan of God with the understanding that there is a different basis for determining one's salvation and one's status as an overcomer. While the basis for the eternal salvation of all born again believers is completely and solely by grace through faith, the status as overcomers, the reception of rewards subsequent to our earthly walk, and the privilege of "reigning with Christ" during His millennial reign is completely and solely by works. Simply put, it is the understanding that grace is for salvation and works are for reward and kingdom privileges. It is also the understanding that neither a lack of "good works" nor any "works of the flesh" can cause a child of God to forfeit his salvation but do result in discipline, punishment and a loss of rewards during and after the earthly state.

I have provided a short synopsis of each chapter with the hope that the reader can get a feel for the urgency and necessity of understanding this highly controversial but opportune subject.

1. The scandalous nature of grace

In this chapter, I have included several biblical and prophetic examples to show the radical and seemingly scandalous nature of grace. Grace is truly a concept that the "world" cannot understand.

2. Grace vs. Works

In this chapter, I present and contrast the principle scriptures for the Calvinistic and Arminian positions and attempt to show how they are in reality two different foundations for two different doctrines and not opposing views for the basis of salvation. I attempt to show the futility of trying to uncover the biblical basis for salvation by synthesizing these two doctrines. I believe that we can make a case for the view that Calvinism is useful for emphasizing the doctrine of grace as it relates to salvation and Arminianism is useful for emphasizing good works as they relate to sanctification and that these are both major but not intersecting doctrines.

3. The kingdom factor

In this chapter, I present and illustrate what I call the "the missing link" of the grace vs. works debate. Christians almost universally believe that the new birth gives each Christian the privilege of reigning with Christ during His millennial reign. Unless we as Christians understand the purpose of this dispensation, we will have a very rude awakening at the return of Christ.

4. Salvation and the kingdom

In this chapter, I present several biblical passages that show several distinctions that the Scriptures make between the principles that determine the eternal salvation of the child of God and the principles that govern the experience of the child of God in the age of the Kingdom of Heaven. I hope to demonstrate among other things that the phrase *weeping and gnashing of teeth* is not a description of the pains of hell but of the discipline of born again Christians during the millennial period.

5. A biblical view of rewards

In this chapter I seek to show how the Bible teaches that God, although no respecter of persons does see the nature, quality and amount of our good works. In this chapter, I seek to show how and why the bible teaches the necessity of good works alongside the grace of God. The grace is for saving us but the works are for rewards, and position in the kingdom.

6. The race, the fight, and the crown

In this chapter I seek to show that many of the metaphors that are usually understood as speaking of salvation and how to get to heaven in reality are speaking of reward and status in the Millennial Kingdom of Christ.

7. The fear of the Lord and holiness

In this chapter, I explore how God deals with us as servants and how this relationship produces holiness to escape the consequences of being a wicked and slothful servant. An unbeliever is not even a wicked and slothful servant but a servant of Satan. There are three kinds of servants in the spiritual realm: good and faithful servants of God, wicked and slothful servants of God and the servants of Satan.

8. The center of God's heart and the vision of the overcomer

In this chapter, I attempt to identify the eternal purpose of God for man from the pages of the Holy Scriptures and show how this eternal purpose relates to the need for each child of God be an overcomer.

9. Building a spiritual inheritance

In this chapter, I suggest a scriptural framework for a life of investment in the kingdom age. This includes a practical earthly plan for a kingdom inheritance through spiritual reproduction. I also offer a panoramic view of discipleship and spiritual parenting in this chapter.

10. The kingdom parables of Matthew 13

In this final chapter, I offer an analysis of the parables of the 13th Chapter of Matthew through which Jesus explained veiled principles of the kingdom of heaven to His disciples. The true meaning of these parables escapes the understanding of the great majority of Christians just as they did the multitudes to which Jesus preached.

CONTENTS

CHAPTER 1

THE SCANDALOUS NATURE OF GRACE

I remember several years ago hearing Rush Limbaugh, a conservative talk radio host tell his listeners that "words mean things". That phrase stayed with me over the years because it is so common for people to treat words as if they have no definite meaning and can easily be exchanged for any number of other terms. One example of this is the way the word grace is used by many Christians. Most Christians agree that the salvation of God through the sacrifice of His son Jesus Christ is based on grace as opposed to works. However, when they develop their theology of salvation they often cloud the true meaning of the word grace.

Words do mean things and it is no accident that the New Testament was originally written in Koine Greek; an extremely rich language often with several different words carrying slight shades of different meaning all translated into a single "one size fits all" English expression. It is of fundamental importance that we understand the meaning of the word grace and that we remain consistent in applying its use in relation to salvation.

Grace from the Greek *"charis"* specifically means undeserved or unmerited favor. For grace to be grace it should never be expected since it has no basis on merit or recompense. Grace is receiving without having a reason to receive, for once there is a reason, it becomes something else.

While my wife Sandra and I were on vacation for our 25th wedding anniversary we were walking along the beachfront on the Atlantic coastal city of Maceió in northeastern Brazil. While we were walking past some new hotels, a tall hansom young man that looked like some kind of security guard or beach patrolman stopped us and asked us if we would like a chance to win a free dinner at the new hotel. He gave me a scratch card and told me that if I rubbed off three matching symbols (out of 5) we would win a free dinner. I was able to choose correctly and we won a voucher for the free dinner. We agreed to return at 6:00 p.m. to claim our meal. When we arrived at the hotel we were introduced to a very attractive young woman who asked us to sit down and chat for a while before dinner. She was very nice so we didn't object.

To make a long story short we were pressured into listening to a 50 minute presentation about timeshares in the group of hotels that they represented. At the end we were asked to sign a contract to buy timeshares for the next ten years. I made it clear that I wasn't prepared to sign any contract so finally we were excused and instructed how to claim our free dinner.

The dinner was fine but in the end it wasn't exactly free. This was an example of a free gift that had nothing to do with grace. How can I say that? Well, for one thing we were chosen because we were obviously tourists in the area on vacation. If we had looked like a couple of beggars or gypsies we would have never received the "chance" to win a "free" dinner. I suspect that the scratch card was also rigged to guarantee a win and a chance for the hotel chain to sell one more vacant room in their half full hotel.

For another thing, it was made clear that in order to be shown to the dining room we had to go through the process of hearing their time share spiel. And finally after we declined to "purchase the goods" we were made to feel that we were practically robbing them by going ahead and receiving what was clearly meant to be a small reward for purchasing their product.

If this was truly an example of a "free gift" or a gift of grace, it would be completely independent of any interest the hotel had of making any money. If it was a gift of grace they would have the place full of gypsies and bums that could have been found scattered along the beach front. This is because wherever there is even an ounce of deserving there can be no grace, only payment. That dinner Sandra and I had was not free. We paid for it by listening patiently to a sales pitch for a product that we did not want to purchase, and then when they should have treated us like deserving patrons, we were made to feel like opportunistic cheapskates!

The truth is that grace is a difficult concept for us humans to comprehend and even more so, to accept. As I stated at the beginning of the chapter many Christians believe that salvation has been given on the basis of grace, but then they turn around and apply principles of barter and exchange to interpret how eternal life and salvation are obtained.

The principle way this is done is by maintaining that there is the possibility that salvation can be lost, due to negligence, disinterest or any other type of sin. Some call it backsliding, others call it "falling away" or "falling from grace."

This reveals either a lack of understanding of what grace really is, or a practical admission that salvation really isn't received on the basis of grace and is somehow paid for by good works and service.

It can be correctly stated that grace only flows down. In other words grace can only be shown to someone who is in a position of need and incapable of repaying what is received. Therefore we can never extend grace to someone who is able to give back what we give. If we could somehow repay the gift of eternal life it would no longer be a gift but simply a kind of loan. Grace is neither God's payment of a debt nor is it His over payment of a debt

Suppose that I have a neighbor with a mischievous son who routinely "borrows" his father's car for "driving practice". One day he decides to borrow his father's car for a joy ride. As soon as he pulls out of the driveway he loses control and crashes into the wall of my front yard and breaks a big hole in it. I can deal with the situation by having one of three different attitudes, justice, mercy or grace. All three are valid attitudes and I would be correct in choosing any of the three.

One way I can deal with the situation is with an attitude of justice: so I explain to the boy that he or his father will have to pay for the damage. The damaged car can be sold and the difference can be used to fix my wall. There would be nothing wrong with this since it is based on what is just and right. The boy and his family need to right the wrong committed against me. Paying for the damage is the right thing for him to do.

Another way that the situation could be resolved is if I looked at the young man and told him that he was already in enough trouble. I could tell him that his father did not have the means to pay for the damage to the car much less repair my wall. I could then have an attitude of mercy and send him away telling him that I will take care of the damage that he caused to my wall and he would take care of the rest of the damage to his father's car. This would be mercy, a little better for him than justice, but he still has the problem of his father's wrecked car.

But there is a third possibility, I can be gracious to him. How would this work out? I could run to the car and ask the boy if he was hurt. He might answer "no, but the car is wrecked and I destroyed your wall." I could then brush those details aside and say, "so you want to learn how to drive, is that right? Listen you don't have to do this behind your father's back. Look, I will fix my wall and pay for the repairs to your father's car. While your car is being fixed, you can use my car, and I myself will teach you how to drive, and once you learn how to drive I will give you my car so that you won't ever have to borrow your father's car again."

Do you know anyone who would treat you that way? Well, God did! That is what God in Christ has done for every sinner. Mankind deserves a one way ticket to hell for what he has done with the life that God has given to be lived out for Him. But instead of treating us with justice, instead of just showing mercy, He showed us grace. He sent His own son to die in our place and then He gave us a position in His own family and called us by His own name, and gave us a share in the inheritance that He reserved for His only begotten son. Grace is surprising, grace is unexpected, grace is divine and because of this, man has a hard time understanding it and how it can be applied to his situation.

Many Christians do not yet understand the greatness of God's grace. It just seems too incredible to them. The world knows so little of the principle of the grace and the gifts of God. We humans instinctively learn to "wheel and deal" and bargain. All day long our minds are occupied with how much work we do and how much we receive for our work. We believe that we have to somehow deserve what we get. Even a lazy freeloader thinks he deserves something just because he is a "have not". We have witnessed the emergence and growth of the "give me" generation of Americans that somehow think that their parents or the Government, or the credit institutions have the obligation to take care of their every need. Their "work" is being needy, and suffering depravation of their heart's desires. Either way, whether rugged individualists like we used to be or, social victims as many have become, we all have a notion of what is due us. For years and years we have invested our lives, time and energy and we are looking for a return on our investment.

We see our lives as a series of deals. Since we have learned to live this way, we also think that God's grace and eternal life are obtained by the same principles. When we hear, understand and receive the Gospel, we come to see the light and in that moment we perceive that grace is free and not a question of bargaining. When this happens there are no thoughts of celebrating grace by continuing in sin since every true believer has received the Spirit of God and God's Spirit within us hates all sin. It is possible, and demonstratively happens quite frequently, that the believer loses his sensitivity and allows sin to remain in his life and goes through the experience that the apostle Paul described in Romans chapter 7. That is why the Spirit of God inspired him to continue with what was written in Chapter 8 of Romans. Many people still haven't been freed from the erroneous concept that the grace of God is a loan to us. They think that if they don't behave in just the right way, that God will ask for His gift of grace back.

Some people have concerns about preaching the grace of God, and without a doubt there has been a lot of misunderstanding about the place of grace in our Christian walk. Some argue that if a person believes that salvation is wholly by grace completely apart from works claiming that if one is "once saved, always saved", he will certainly sin more freely. This can be considered the most common and strongest argument against the teaching of salvation exclusively by grace or what is often called "eternal security". If a person knows that he is eternally saved won't he easily become lazy and start to commit all types of sin? Isn't such a teaching quite dangerous to one's holiness?

The answer is "no" if we are talking about a born again believer, a true son of God. I have two sons. Suppose that I tell each of them that since they have become my sons they will always be my children, for all eternity. Upon hearing this, who would guess that they would become so happy and relieved that I would never throw them out of the house or disown them as sons that they would start destroying everything in sight, breaking windows, throwing down plates and overturning tables ripping up books, parading their friends through the house and in general breaking every rule that they have ever understood as being law in our home? Would they act this way just because there would be no danger of them being kicked out of the family? If they should do such a thing I would doubt that they were really my sons. I would suspect that some aliens took over their bodies and possessed them.

Our sons no longer live with us, but I do not believe they ever doubted that they would always be our sons. Of course when they were younger they had to be punished to learn good behavior. Just as God disciplines and punishes every son He receives, I disciplined my own sons. Hebrews 12:5-7 states:

> *And you have forgotten the exhortation which speaks to you as to sons: "My son, do not despise the chastening of the Lord, Nor be discouraged when you are rebuked by Him; For whom the Lord loves He chastens, And scourges every son whom He receives." If you endure chastening, God deals with you as with sons; for what son is there whom a father does not chasten?*

Eternal security doesn't mean that God doesn't discipline His disobedient children. My sons learned to behave and become decent young men, actually I am proud to say, very well behaved young men (my wife and I often receive compliments on how well behaved they are). But that is not because I would threaten to disown them if they misbehaved. I did threaten to discipline them, and most of the time I followed through with my threats. Many a time I hurt my right hand on their rear ends, that is when I couldn't find a belt (they would hide the belts). Quite honestly many times I felt like throttling their little necks. Several times my older son resisted me so vehemently that I invited him to look for another place to live. I had to tell him that there was no possibility for me to allow him to continue to live in our home if he wanted to set the rules. Thank God that he came to his senses and realized that premature independence sucks! He obtained instant wisdom. No place to live, no food to eat, no electricity to plug his guitar into, no wheels to go places . . . suddenly mom and dad's place became a really cool place to live! But oh how I feared that he would bolt!

I remembered the parable of the prodigal son. He told his father "I am outta here" Except this father, was way, way more generous than I ever was. He gave his kid his inheritance; the ungrateful brat didn't even have the decency to wait for his father to die. That would be like my son telling me that he didn't like the way I ran things at the house and suggested that I rent him a penthouse, buy some "hot" wheels for him to drive around with and give him a nice big savings account to pay for his new lifestyle. Fat chance! But, you see, that is grace. You may even feel it is unwise and imprudent, but that is the main message of the parable.

We can insist on our own way with God and even take that which He has blessed us with for the purpose of doing His will and use it for our own purposes. If that happens He may say that we were once alive and now we are dead (eating pig food) but we would still be His sons. In the parable the prodigal returned planning to serve his father as a slave rather than as a son. But the father treated the undeserving son with nothing but grace.

Yes my friend, in the eyes of the older brother, and quite possibly in your eyes, this father was rewarding the rebelliousness and ungratefulness of his son. He threw a party and declared that "this my son was dead, and now he is alive!" Do you think for a minute that the next day the son was back to his old tricks because he discovered that his father was a sucker for forgetting the past and not only forgiving him but piling on His richest blessings to such an undeserving ingrate of a son?

And even if the son didn't repent, and the next day he demanded another fortune from his father just as before what might his father's reaction be? Just imagine the ensuing scene: "Listen old man that was a nice party and all, but I just can't take it anymore, I need my freedom, I want to go back to my old friends. I'm outta here again. How much you got left to give me?" Would his father throw his check book on the ground and rant, "that is it!"? "I have had it. Get out of here! You go to hell you ungrateful bastard! After all I have done for you, you repay my love with this?" That might be my reaction or your reaction, and perhaps it wouldn't even be a wrong or improper reaction, but it wouldn't be grace because grace works independently of reciprocity.

Oh this grace of God is so beyond our understanding! I love my sons tremendously, but I could never picture myself being so gracious. Praise God that He is not like me! I can't reject the teaching of eternal security just because I am not so inclined to show the same degree of grace that God does. Any person that could rejoice in the grace of God by sinning just because he knows that he can get away with it only shows that he was never a son of God in the first place. We as the sons of God, do sin! We do fail! If we deny our sin, God calls us liars. While sin in our born again life will adversely affect our fellowship with the Father, because of His graciousness, it never affects our status as His begotten sons.

I now have absolutely no fear of losing my salvation; formerly however that was definitely an issue for me. At the same time, I can honestly say that in spite of ridding myself of the fear of losing my salvation I have more desire than ever before to be holy and free of all forms of sin.

The grace in the life of a child of God isn't experienced as a function of downplaying or excusing sin but as a function of enhancing the experience of our holiness and the power of God for fruitful ministry. Paul stated that the grace of God worked through him more that all the others. He certainly wasn't saying that he got away with more sin that the rest of the apostles. Those who think differently just "don't get it". It isn't easy to "get" grace or understand grace, it's divine for God's sake!

CHAPTER 2

GRACE VS. WORKS

I grew up in a denomination that has the following phrase stated in its doctrinal statement. "We believe that the gift of eternal life is a present possession of every true disciple of Jesus Christ, and that nothing or any person can take it from him. However, it is a realistic possibility, for a true believer, once saved, of his own free will to no longer "continue in the faith" but instead to apostatize, "depart from the faith" return to sin, and consequently forfeit the eternal life he once possessed."

Never has anyone pressured me to hold either position for or against the possibility of forfeiting or losing one's salvation. On the contrary, as a young Christian within the denomination, I had always assumed that there were proponents for, as well as against "eternal security". I somehow imagined that there was no definite position on the matter.

It was only after I left for the foreign mission field that I noticed that the phrase "We believe that it is a realistic possibility, for a true believer to forfeit the eternal life he once possessed", was included in the doctrinal statement. To say that there is a possibility that we can forfeit eternal life is, in practice, no different that stating that there is a possibility that we can lose it. If we can forfeit something, then it is not permanent, it is not secure.

If someone were to hold a gun to your head and force you to renounce your faith, or to forfeit your salvation, if that were possible, you would lose it. I used to teach that while the bible teaches that nothing can separate us from the Love of God we ourselves can depart and turn our backs on God. In other words, we cannot lose our salvation but we can throw it away. Let us be honest, if we can throw something away, it is not secure. Eternal security states that salvation cannot be lost, thus the position that there is a possibility however distinct or remote of losing it, is the same as stating that salvation can be lost and that eternal security does not exist and is a lie.

As I began to dedicate more time to the study of the Word, I consolidated my conviction that there does appear to be more scriptural passages to support the rejection of Eternal Security than the acceptance of it. For years in my pulpit ministry, I pounded away at what I considered "false hopes" of church members who could not seem to get out of bondage to sin.

I now see these poor souls as "defeated Christians" and even practicing "apostates" but not "lost" or reverted to an unregenerate state. I have come to see that the logical end of the arguments that I was using is that hardly anyone may realistically expect to make it to heaven, or at least it is extremely difficult to both receive salvation and keep it. Let me offer some examples to justify this position. Let us start with the words of Christ in the Sermon on the Mount.

In Matthew 5:20 Jesus stated:

> *"For I say to you, that unless your righteousness exceeds the righteousness of the scribes and Pharisees, you will by no means enter the kingdom of heaven."*

He stated this after saying that He did not come to take away any part of the Law, but that He came to fulfill all of it. The practical outworking of this declaration is that unless our "works of righteousness" outshine those of the Pharisees we would never qualify to enter the kingdom of heaven. Granted, many Pharisees were corrupt but they were men who prayed often, fasted regularly, tithed faithfully and meticulously obeyed the commands of the law. What can we say about the accepted pattern of the modern day Christian who confesses Christ and appeals to grace to cover his failings? Does he pray often? Does he fast ever? Does he tithe faithfully and correctly? Is he truly a student of the scriptures? These are the very things that Christ was laying out as requirements for entering the Kingdom of Heaven!

Certainly, He was not referring to their piety of heart, since He often exposed them as hypocrites. Many of the Pharisees were religious in their practices but lacked a heart for God, although not all of them because Paul was devout and really believed that he was serving God before he had his conversion experience. If we are to understand that Christ was speaking of salvation here, then however we state it, we must make it clear that no one will make it into heaven who does not maintain a strict regime of works of righteousness. Yet how can we rightly divide this scripture with the words of Titus 3:5: "not by works of righteousness which we have done, but according to His mercy He saved us, through the washing of regeneration and renewing of the Holy Spirit." To be fair and honest with both texts we would have to combine the two somehow. We could state it something like this: We do not initially receive salvation by any act of righteousness of our own, but if indeed we do receive salvation, at any given moment there must be enough practical works of righteousness manifested in our life, sufficient to out-shine any devout Pharisee, in order that we may enter the kingdom of heaven. I would estimate that over 90% of those who confess Christ, according to His apparent qualification, would in His words, in no case enter into the kingdom of heaven.

In Matthew 7:21 Jesus stated

> *"Not everyone who says to Me, 'Lord, Lord,' shall enter the kingdom of heaven, but he who does the will of My Father in heaven."*

Who can honestly say at any, and I mean any moment, that he or she is doing the will of God? Many of those who claim to be Christians do not even have much of an idea of what God's will is. Doing the will of the Father implies knowing what the will of the Father is. What is the will of the Father? . . . Well, how about "being holy as He is holy", that is His will, right? Ask yourself this question: "Are you as holy as God?" That is what He requires.

What about God not being willing that any should perish but that all repent? How shall they hear unless you or I preach? What about you, are you a preacher of the Gospel? Do you obey the great commission? Do you love the Lord with all your heart, soul and mind? I said, with all your heart, soul and mind. . . . No? Yet that is what God commands. How can any of us enter into the kingdom of heaven with these kinds of requirements? You may argue that of course God does not expect us to be perfect. I agree, although He does command us to be perfect.

So now, we have a dilemma. How much perfection is enough? How good is good enough? If we rightly say that God does not look at our own righteousness or works for our salvation, but those of Christ, we should then admit that our salvation would not be lost, based on our performance if God looks at Christ's works and not ours. Because if we do not, then we must admit that at some point God no longer considers Christ's work and begins to consider our own work, and that there is a certain line that if passed, will cause us to forfeit our salvation. And unless we can define that line or limit, then we are no better off than many Catholics, who hope that they are good enough to be saved but never expect to ever be able to know if they are saved or not.

You see, if the maintenance of our salvation is up to us, then there must be a measurable defining point beyond which we can know if we are "in" or "out" of eternal life. If the Lord is not wholly responsible to keep us saved, then we must be able to answer the question: what sin or sins or whatever, is effective to exclude us from eternal life. This is no small matter. It is a matter of life or death, more exactly of eternal life or eternal damnation. There is no other need more important or urgent than this.

I want to present some questions that suggest keys to unraveling these doubts. I will discuss these questions in later portions of this book. For now, I think they may be helpful for further meditation.

- Does God explicitly reveal the basis for man's salvation, if so, what is this basis?

- Is it possible and helpful to distinguish the source and means for our salvation from the basis of our salvation?

- Are the true signs of the new birth heart attitudes or external acts or both?

- Can true Christians fail in performance and yet retain their salvation?

- Is the kingdom of heaven necessarily the same thing as heaven and eternal life?

- Are there passages that speak of Christian discipline that may be confused with passages that speak of eternal damnation?

I would like to continue by clarifying my motives for writing this book. I have no academic interests to fulfill by theologizing about the grace/works debate. I feel driven by mission and the need to see the great commission fulfilled and the salvation of the generation of which I am part. While it may not be immediately evident how this subject ties in with getting the great commission accomplished, nevertheless that is my motivation. By the end of this book, my hope and prayer is to energize those who read these chapters to work the works of God out of holy fear and trembling and out of the love, which God has shed upon our hearts for His will and the lost.

I also would like to preface further statements in later chapters by saying that I have no doubt at all that many, many people will be eternally lost in the fire of hell despite the great love and grace of God. God's offer of salvation is free and ridiculously generous, but those who pass it up will suffer unimaginable, indescribable and eternal torment with no hope of ever having another chance of taking up God's generous offer.

Because of the weight of scripture interpreted under the rules of hermeneutics, I purport that the salvation that God gives to man is for eternity and that there is no possibility for the true Christian to perish in eternal damnation once he has received eternal life. This is not to say that God will not punish Christians, or that He will not judge or withhold reward from an unfaithful believer. If a Christian has unrepentant sin in his life eventually, God will discipline him and he will suffer punishment at the judgment seat of Christ. Yet I believe that the bible teaches that a Christian cannot "lose" his salvation. I believe that the scriptures teach that once God saves us, we are eternally saved.

At this point I would like to ask the reader to refrain from "jumping ahead" and considering the apparently negative implications of a perfectly free and no restrictions offer of eternal salvation. This subject is highly charged and there are apparent contradictions. It takes real emotional effort and stability to go through each argument without feeling manipulated. I speak from experience because that is how I felt as I dealt with each line of thinking. The difference for me now is that I have a scriptural basis for harmonizing so many passages that formerly seemed contradictory or at least antagonistic to each other.

I would like to present nine biblical arguments to support the position that man receives salvation exclusively by grace, that salvation is eternal and thus un-losable. Biblical scholars have been using the first eight of these arguments for years and I will revisit them. I have developed a ninth argument that I have never seen used before and I imagine that more can be put forth as the whole of Scripture is considered further concerning this matter.

SALVATION IS A GIFT OF GOD

All born again Christian know that God gives salvation based on His grace. It is a gift of God. Our own merits and works have nothing to do with God's gift of salvation by grace.

Since God gives salvation by grace, then, we can never be debtors before God in relation to this free salvation after having received the gift. If I show grace to someone, I cannot wait for any repayment. If I give a gift to someone and have any thought of them repaying me, or of reclaiming the gift, then it would be a loan and not a gift and thus not grace.

If God gives us salvation with the hope of later receiving from us any good work, even the works of faith, then it would not be a gift of grace. Whatever is given by grace cannot be repaid. The bible clearly states that salvation is a gift or present of God.

> *For the wages of sin is death, but the gift of God is eternal life in Christ Jesus our Lord. Romans 6:23*

> *For by grace you have been saved through faith, and that not of yourselves; it is the gift of God, not of works, lest anyone should boast. Ephesians 2:8-9*

Death here means primarily spiritual death. Death is payment for something earned. Spiritual death is the payment for the works of sin. The justice of God determines that the unbelieving sinner be paid his wages. But the Grace of God determines that the sinner who believes that Christ took upon Himself the sin of all mankind and received the just payment for mankind's sin doesn't have to collect the wages of sin and is free to accept the gift of God of eternal life. Now eternal life is not payment for anything. Faith is not a wage that we can pay to deserve eternal life. If faith were wages for salvation then eternal life would not be a gift. Notice that Romans 6:23 contrasts wages with gift.

Paul did not teach that the wages of sin is death and the wages of faith is eternal life. The gift of God is eternal life; therefore, it is not possible to lose an eternal life that God gave by grace. God doesn't give us something to later ask for it back, or to later take it back because we didn't meet certain conditions. We can collect a loan, but we cannot reclaim something we give by grace. If God gave us eternal life by grace, then He cannot reclaim it. Therefore, we can never lose our salvation or our eternal life.

God is eternal and unchangeable. Once He gives us something, He never asks for it back. God never asks to borrow anything from us, nor does He loan anything. He just gives, and expects us to give as well. God did not give us eternal life to "buy" our devotion to Him. If we do not freely "give" ourselves as holy sacrifices, even though we were created by Him, and bought by Him, and we are by right His property, He will not take by force that which is rightfully His. He asks us to give ourselves, as sacrifices. A sacrifice is given.

God saved us because of His love. This is clear from John 3:16

> For God so loved the world that He gave His only begotten Son, that whoever believes in Him should not perish but have everlasting life.

If when we were sinners God loved us to the point of giving us the life of His Son, could it be possible for God to reject someone after conversion that becomes weak or inconsistent? The love of God does not change and neither does His grace.

There is no change in the love with which God loves man. If the possibility of a believer losing his salvation existed then there would be the possibility of a change in God. By God's own definition of Himself that is not possible.

When God gave His own Son as our savior, we need to recognize that He gave that which is more important than eternal life (His own Son).

> He who did not spare His own Son, but delivered Him up for us all, how shall He not with Him also freely give us all things? Romans 8:32

> For if when we were enemies we were reconciled to God through the death of His Son, much more, having been reconciled, we shall be saved by His life. Romans 5:10

If God wished to freely give us His Son to pay the price of our sins while we were still His enemies, would He think of denying us eternal life at some later point based on our performance or lack of it? Since God was willing to give eternal life to those who were formerly His enemies, would He not even be more willing to preserve the eternal life of His own begotten sons? Are we to believe that keeping our eternal life is more difficult than receiving it in the first place? Or does this God of grace seek to save the sinner only to continue to threaten him with the weight of all his responsibilities to maintain this wonderful salvation that he supposedly received freely by grace?

Imagine for a moment if God said to you and to each person who comes to Him for salvation: "*O.K. now I saved you, now don't blow it, you don't have an unlimited number of chances for error. Most people will never make it all the way to heaven but I have given you a chance. You may never know at any point if you will make all the way, so do not lose faith. Otherwise things could be even worse than before.*" Just think how your kids would turn out if you raised them that way.

Once God gave His only begotten Son how could He deny us our salvation? Salvation is nothing compared to the value of the Son of God.

God gave us His Son and gave us salvation, if He does not reclaim His Son why would He reclaim salvation? Therefore, according to the grace and love of God it is impossible to lose our salvation.

SALVATION IS A PREDETERMINED GIFT OF GOD

The salvation that God offers was not an afterthought, but a purposeful, planned act.

> *For whom He foreknew, He also predestined to be conformed to the image of His Son, that He might be the firstborn among many brethren. Moreover whom He predestined, these He also called; whom He called, these He also justified; and whom He justified, these He also glorified. Romans 8:29-30*

When God saved us He also justified us, however God knew us way before that, our justification came much later. This passage in Romans is a chain of which the first link is His foreknowledge. The second link is our predestination. The third, is our calling and the fourth is our justification finally the fifth being our glorification. We think that we knew God when we were justified, but God already knew us. In addition, those that God knew, He marked. He marked us to be identical to Jesus. He is not content to have just one son, but desires that we all become sons in the image of His first begotten Son Jesus.

Our history with God began way before the day of our conversion when we were justified, but began in God's presence in eternity past. If we could lose our salvation, it would be a matter of God's omniscience. If He knew that at one point that He would save us, how could we not be saved at a later point?

God cannot change our justification without affecting His foreknowledge, predestination and calling. God is the beginning and the end, the alpha and omega (Revelation 22:13). We begin things and we try to finish them, but we do not always succeed. God however is not like us: He finishes what He begins. The work that God begins will not stop midway. Salvation is a work of God, not a human work. God saved us He will complete the work He began in us.

> *. . . being confident of this very thing, that He who has begun a good work in you will complete it until the day of Jesus Christ; Philippians 1:6*

If salvation could stop halfway in our lives that would mean that God declined to finish what He began. Either He stopped it or man stopped it. Either way God's character would make this impossible. He began His work of salvation in us in the foreknowledge that He would perform it to completion and lead us to glorification.

I believe that we can affirm that our salvation is eternally secure because it is a work of God. If it depended on us, we would fail, but just as God was responsible for beginning the work, He is also responsible for preserving it.

In Philippians 1:6, Paul is confident (completely convinced in his spirit) that God would complete or fulfill the work (that work, which we will yet define and examine) which He had begun in the Philippian believers.

We can safely deduce that the work that God began in these believers in general began even before they were born, and then more explicitly upon their conversion. What may not be so clear to all is when He will complete it.

I used to think that the time that God works in our lives was limited to the time that we are living here on earth in this present age. I have even preached this verse accordingly several times. Thus, I rendered the phrase "until the day of Jesus Christ" as meaning until the end of life on this earth which most likely would be before the day of Jesus Christ.

In other words, God will finish what He began by the end of your life. That sounds wonderful and comforting but neither reflects the historical narrative of scripture nor common experience. Most all Christians know of at least one deceased believing brother or sister in whose life here on earth God had not finished His work. There are countless examples of people who started well in their walk with Christ but fell away and by the end of their lives could hardly be identified by fruit in their experience as true Christians much less as someone within whom the work of God has been completed and fulfilled.

The Philippians had not begun this work, God had. Paul based his assurance that God would fulfill and complete this work on his confidence that whatever God starts, He also finishes. God is perfect and there is no reason why He would begin such a work only to latter abandon it. He has infinite power to complete it. No enemy could overcome His purpose. No difficulty could prevent Him from completing His good work. Not to do so would go against His very character and it is unthinkable to consider that He will not complete everything that He has initiated. No, God abandons nothing good that He undertakes. While He does mete out discipline from time to time and effect course corrections, He always follows through with what He has purposed.

God has left no un-finished worlds or solar systems. There are no half-made and forsaken works of His hands. There is no evidence in His works of creation of any change of plan, or of having forsaken what He began from disgust, or disappointment, or lack of power to complete what He started. How then could there be such evidence concerning His work in the human heart? If God indeed began a work, any work, in a person then according to this text and the spirit of all scripture He will finish and complete it.

O.k. so, when did God ever do this, and what does His completed work look like in the life of one of His children? As stated above God planned us in eternity past when He foreknew us, the Apostle Paul inspired by the Holy Spirit calls us His workmanship. There are ample examples throughout the Scriptures that show us that God prepares each one of His children that He foreknew and predestined them to be conformed to the image of His Son. God is great enough to leave no detail to chance. God somehow divinely chooses and puts together through the free will of each generation the people and circumstances so that each child of God is born into the world to the parents and in the location and circumstances that He has predetermined.

God began His work in us even before our parents conceived us. Even before conversion, God has planned and ordained our life circumstances to play a part in the mosaic that contributes toward His purposes. God began His work in each of His children before they took on an earthly body and one day He will finish this work.

There are many examples of this in the Word but the most classic is Jacob. Jacob apparently started out all wrong. Even at birth, he was trying to usurp his brother's rightful place as firstborn. Jacob was a lying, conniving, manipulative soul who for some strange and wonderful reason became one of the most used men of God. At the end of his life, marked by the discipline of many years he grew and matured into the noble man of God called Israel. What a contrast with what he was in the beginning. The presence of this patriarch who had wrestled with God and obtained His blessing impressed even Pharaoh, king of the most powerful nation on earth at the time.

We can safely say that God finished the work that He began in Jacob's life. He is one of the heroes of faith mentioned in Hebrews 11. God taught him a thing or two about spiritual vision, for so many years he wandered through life's desert not understanding what God was doing in his life. But at the end when he prophesied over his sons and his son Joseph saw that he placed his right hand on Ephraim instead of Manasseh the firstborn, when he tried to correct him, his father said that he knew who was who, but that the younger would be greater than the firstborn.

However, just as we have examples of men and women who saw the work of God fulfilled in their lives we also have examples of those who apparently did not see the work of God completed in their time here on earth. Are we to conclude that this host of imperfect and admittedly fallible men and women were eternally lost? What of Esau, he was a carnal man but had more character than Jacob once had. Saul worried about his image and never learned how to follow his spiritual leader but he did not involve himself in scandalous sins like those that David did (lying, adultery, murder). We can also cite the example of Ananias and Saphira. God Himself cut their lives short. Are we to understand that because they lied to the Holy Spirit about the price of their offering that they lost their salvation or that God never began a work in their lives? I shudder to think that someone could be eternally lost because of one act of dishonesty or hypocrisy.

What about you dear reader, what has yet to be fulfilled in your life? If you died today, could you say that God finished the work that He began in your life? Unless you recognize that God has feats for you to conquer through your faith, quite realistically you will not accomplish much of any eternal worth before your time comes to leave this world. Then how will God have completed His work in you?

To answer this question, consider three possibilities: First, God never started a work in you. Second, He started it and then gave up, or third, He started it and will finish it before the day of Jesus Christ.

I believe that we can boldly affirm that what God begins He finishes. Your challenge is to cooperate with Him now so that He can conclude His work before you leave this life. Otherwise, you will suffer lost at the judgment seat of Christ. Then by the end of the Millennium, He will have completed His work in your life, but it will not be a very pleasant experience.

Salvation Implies That We Are Begotten Children of God

It is of extreme importance that we recognize just what kind of salvation have we received. Salvation is a work of regeneration, or in other words, we receive the very life of God.

> *But as many as received Him, to them He gave the right to become children of God, to those who believe in His name: John 1:12*

We are born of God. We receive the power to become His sons. We have been born again by the Spirit of God.

> *Whoever believes that Jesus is the Christ is born of God, and everyone who loves Him who begot also loves him who is begotten of Him. 1 John 5:1*

When a sinner believes in the Lord Jesus, he receives salvation and God gives him new life. We know then that God begat us. We are now His sons. How can this relationship be undone?

If you have a bad, rebellious and undisciplined son you could deny him in a court of law, but he continues to be your son. An evil son is also born of his father. He shares the same life as a member of the family. The same occurs between God and us. We receive the power to become sons. Even if we become disobedient and undisciplined we are still sons of God, it is a question of nature and relationship. There is no way to change this.

The only way to terminate the relationship between father and son is through the death of one of the two. We know that God cannot die and now that we have received eternal life, spiritual death has no power over us.

After Adam sinned, God placed a cherub with a flaming sword at the entrance of the garden thus preventing him from eating of the tree of life and living eternally.

> *Then the Lord God said, "Behold, the man has become like one of Us, to know good and evil. And now, lest he put out his hand and take also of the tree of life, and eat, and live forever" Genesis 3:22*

Born again Christians today are the redeemed sons and daughters of God. Today we eat of the true tree of Life, which is Christ Jesus, and therefore we receive eternal life and will live eternally. This is a fact that we cannot change.

The truth is that we are more sons of God than Adam was. God did not beget Adam. Adam was God's creature. He was no more God's son than Frankenstein's monster was the son of Frankenstein. God created Adam from the dust of the earth, but Christians are born into God's family as sons not just as God's creation.

Jesus Christ was formerly the only begotten son of God. Because of the cross, He became the first born of many brethren. The only way to enter into God's family is through the new birth. Because God begat us we are heirs of God. God has no adopted children, He begat them all through the new birth by the Spirit. When the Bible teaches about "adoption" as sons, we need to understand that the term did not mean adoption in the way that we understand it today. The word translated in the Bible as adoption in modern English denoted the passage of a begotten son that formerly as a child had been treated with fewer privileges than a slave, but later on had become a mature son having full access to his father's estate. So once again, spiritual birth because of its nature is irreversible. No son can become unborn! No child of God can find himself out of the family. Once born into the family one becomes a permanent member of the family. Whether distant or near, good or bad, grateful or bitter, God has all kinds of Children with all kinds of attitudes.

It is true that God has His pattern. He expects His Children to reflect His divine characteristics, yet many do not, and the truth is that to some extent, all fail. The Word of God teaches that he who claims to be without sin deceives himself and the truth is not in him (1John 1:8).

It is very difficult for the religious mind to accept the doctrine of sonship. If our position as sons depended on our faithfulness and capacity to endure until the end, then God's choice of metaphor, the symbol of the relationship between Himself and His people would have been tragically inadequate. Only the God of Christianity reveals Himself as "Father". This is strikingly significant.

SALVATION IMPLIES THAT WE ARE MEMBERS OF THE BODY OF CHRIST.

When someone receives salvation, God not only regenerates them but He makes them one spirit with Him (1Cor. 6:17). Beyond that, they also become members of His body.

> But he who is joined to the Lord is one spirit with Him. 1Corinthians 6:17

> Now you are the body of Christ, and members individually. 1Cor. 12:27

> Do you not know that your bodies are members of Christ? Shall I then take the members of Christ and make them members of a harlot? Certainly not! 1Corinthians 6:15

When a sinner converts, he not only receives regeneration and eternal life, but God also unites him to the body of Christ in order to become a member of His body. If it were possible to later perish and be lost, that would be the same as mutilating the body of Christ. There would be one less member, a hand, finger, nose or other member. The body of Christ is not merely an illustration; it is a definite spiritual reality, not a physical connection but a spiritual bond that transcends time and space.

And if one member suffers, all the members suffer with it; or if one member is honored, all the members rejoice with it. 1 Corinthians 12:26

SALVATION IMPLIES THAT WE ARE LIVING STONES OF GOD'S HOUSE

When individual Christians gather in one place, they become the temple of God. Every believer is like a stone of this building and the Lord Jesus is the foundation. He is the corner stone and we are smaller stones built up together by Him.

. . . you also, as living stones, are being built up a spiritual house, a holy priesthood, to offer up spiritual sacrifices acceptable to God through Jesus Christ. 1 Peter 2:5

If there were the possibility of a believer losing his salvation then the spiritual temple of God would be full of missing stones and less attractive than an old house. Just imagine if we could see this spiritual reality with our eyes. At any given moment there would be stones removed and others taking their place, there would be an advance but then a regression.

God is a master planner and architect and He has already separated the materials for the edification of His temple. No chosen stone will be lost. Some may take longer to prepare than others before they are laid in place, but none are chose and then discarded.

And the temple, when it was being built, was built with stone finished at the quarry, so that no hammer or chisel or any iron tool was heard in the temple while it was being built. 1 Kings 6:7

Here we have a prophetic illustration of the building of the temple. The artisans cut and prepared the stones on the mountain so that there was no banging or grinding of steel tools. The workers then merely laid the stones in their place.

Can you imagine that Solomon's artisans were more capable of building than God Himself was? Could God make a mistake when He sets a stone in His temple? Could God not know how to calculate the lasting capacity of an individual stone? In the Old Testament, He used men to build, but in the New Testament He is the builder. If we are part of the Temple of God, we cannot be lost.

At this point, I just want to make a statement about analogies and types.

Many people think that an analogy is only useful up until the point that it affirms one's doctrinal position. If at any point the analogy contradicts one's position, it is no longer valid or necessary and can be freely used or discarded as needed. Analogies are neither good nor bad: in general, they are only tools to illustrate a position. The problem is not with analogies, but with faulty teaching. A good analogy of a bad teaching only serves to cloud the understanding. In attempting to refute the teaching of eternal security, I once coined the phrase "nobody is going to analogize their way into heaven" and I still believe that is true. However, God has divinely chosen the examples that He has given us in His Word to teach doctrine so we cannot treat them as just incidental choices to illustrate truth. God calls us sons because that perfectly describes our relationship with Him. And to teach that once we become sons of God we will always be His sons, and thus cannot lose our position as sons as heirs of eternal life is by no means an abuse of the word picture used by God. The same is true when God calls us members of the body and stones of the temple. God did not provide us with these metaphors to obscure meaning but to help us picture the nature of spiritual truths.

SALVATION IMPLIES RECEIVING THE HOLY SPIRIT AS THE SEAL AND EARNEST OF A HEAVENLY INHERITANCE

At the very moment that a person receives his salvation, he receives the seal of the Holy Spirit.

> *In Him you also trusted, after you heard the word of truth, the gospel of your salvation; in whom also, having believed, you were sealed with the Holy Spirit of promise, who is the guarantee of our inheritance until the redemption of the purchased possession, to the praise of His glory. Ephesians 1:13-14*

God does not place the seal of the His Holy Spirit upon a special class of Christians or on those who work especially hard to sanctify themselves. This scripture teaches us that all those who receive the gospel and believe are also sealed.

What does it mean to be sealed? When God saved us, He put His Holy Spirit in us as a seal to mark us indicating that we belong permanently to Him. Suppose that a brother had his name printed on his bible. By doing this, he transfers the image of the impressed stamp onto his bible. This stamp indicates that the bible belongs to him. The seal implies ownership of property. When we believe on the Lord Jesus, God places the stamp of the Holy Spirit on us. God is our owner and we belong to Him.

Once God places His seal on us, no one can remove it, no matter what they do. The seal is a guarantee of authenticity. Those who do not have the Holy Spirit according to Romans 8:9 do not belong to Christ. The presence of the Spirit in the believer is the proof, the seal that he is an authentic son of God. Such a proof is not so much for others as much as for our own benefit of knowing that God has saved us and has given us the inheritance of eternal life. The apostle Paul stated this certainty in his epistle to the church in Rome:

> *The Spirit Himself bears witness with our spirit that we are children of God, Romans 8:16*

The seal will last until the day of redemption; therefore, it is a guarantee that the work will be finished.

> *And do not grieve the Holy Spirit of God, by whom you were sealed for the day of redemption. Ephesians 4:30*

The day of redemption is the day that the Lord will return; it is the day that He will glorify us.

> *Not only that, but we also who have the firstfruits of the Spirit, even we ourselves groan within ourselves, eagerly waiting for the adoption, the redemption of our body. Romans 8:23*

When the Lord returns (not at the rapture, but to set up His kingdom) He will send His angels who will gather all those whom the Holy Spirit has sealed. There is no way to remove the seal of God. Once He has sealed us, there is no turning back. Once the Spirit enters in us, He will never leave us.

> *And I will pray the Father, and He will give you another Helper, that He may abide with you forever John 14:16*

In the Old Testament David prayed that God would not remove His Spirit from him, but in the New Testament, nobody needs to pray this way. Even if the Spirit is grieved in us, He will never leave us.

Today we are the property of God. Since He paid such a high price for us, He will stop at nothing to keep us. If we bought a jewel for a million dollars, we would stop at nothing to guard it. God bought us for the highest price, the blood of Jesus. To God we are His most precious treasure and He will never lose us. The truth is I can't keep or guard myself, even though God has repeatedly commanded me to guard my heart, my mind, my body, keep myself from idols and cling to the things of God, in the final analysis it is God that keeps me and can never lose me.

However, the Holy Spirit is not just the seal of God; He is also the earnest of the promise.

> . . . who also has sealed us and given us the Spirit in our hearts as
> a guarantee. 2Corinthians 1:22

The Bible teaches that the Lord is our inheritance therefore; He has given us the earnest of the Spirit as a guarantee. We will inherit everything that God is as well as everything that He has. The Holy Spirit is the earnest, the guarantee, of the inheritance. When we were born again, we received the promise of God that we would inherit heaven. How can we know that God will not change His mind and give up on us? The answer is because of the earnest that He advanced to us: the Holy Spirit. We cannot lose our salvation because God gave us the Holy Spirit as a guarantee.

SALVATION IMPLIES BECOMING THE FATHER'S GIFT TO JESUS THE SON

God the Father gave those who He saved as a gift to His Son Jesus Christ. We are the Father's gift to the Son.

> "I have manifested Your name to the men whom You have given
> Me out of the world. They were Yours, You gave them to Me, and
> they have kept Your word. John 17:6

If it were possible to lose our salvation the fact that God gave us to Jesus would mean that He was giving a gift that He might later take back: a prospect too far beneath God's dignity and character.

> All that the Father gives Me will come to Me, and the one who
> comes to Me I will by no means cast out. John 6:37

We are not a cheap present nor will the Lord Jesus toss us aside after having received us.

*My Father, who has given them to Me, is greater than all; and no
one is able to snatch them out of My Father's hand. John 10:29*

God did not save us for doing this or that, thus we do not lose our
salvation by doing this or that, or by failing to do this or that. If we
were to fight and try our hardest to save ourselves, it would take just
one small oversight or lack of care and we would be finished. However,
God did not save us in this manner; He saved us entirely by His grace.

We should not think that salvation comes from and begins with the
Lord, but the keeping of it and the finishing of it depends on us. We
could never preserve ourselves in perfection, not even for one day. God
called us to persevere in faith and to keep ourselves unspotted from the
world. Yes, we have a responsibility to do our part in maintaining
fellowship with God, but that is both distinct from and subsequent to
salvation. The work of salvation is all of God. If you are saved today,
you are saved forever. If you can lose your salvation tomorrow, what
worth is any salvation today?

SALVATION IMPLIES THAT GOD KEEPS AND GUARDS US.

God teaches us in His word that He keeps us unto salvation. Four
dimensions of God keep us in His saving hand. These are The Son of
God, the power of God, the promises of God and the Love of God.

THE SON OF GOD KEEPS US: THE LORD JESUS IS OUR HIGH PRIEST

The Lord Jesus is not only our substitute sacrifice; He is also our high
priest. Without the Lord as savior, we would be lost and without hope,
but without the Lord as intercessor we would never persevere.

Only the Lord Jesus as a high priest before God can maintain our
salvation. The only way we can maintain our salvation is because He is
praying and interceding for us.

*Therefore, He is also able to save to the uttermost those who come
to God through Him, since He always lives to make intercession
for them. Hebrews 7:25*

THE POWER OF GOD KEEPS US: HE IS THE ONE THAT KEEPS AND GUARDS US.

The keeping of our salvation does not depend on our believing, but on the protecting and keeping power of God. We do not keep ourselves; God keeps us.

It is by grace through faith that we receive the salvation of God but it is by grace through His power, not our faith, that we receive God's keeping.

> . . . *who are kept by the power of God through faith for salvation ready to be revealed in the last time. 1Peter 1:5*

Do you really think that you are the one that clings to God through your faith, or that it is God who clings to you by His power? To be kept by the power of God means that if it were possible for us to be lost it would not be our fault, but His. Our faith may limit the manifestation of God's power in many things subsequent to salvation but our faith never limits His power to keep us. That is irreverent thinking because God keeps us; therefore, we cannot lose our salvation.

We can divide salvation into three stages. The salvation mentioned here refers to the last stage, glorification. Therefore, the Lord guards us until the end. Salvation is something entirely attributed to God.

If the preservation of our salvation depended upon us, we would not be able to hold onto it even for a few hours, much less for the rest of our life. However, if the Lord Jesus keeps us, then indeed we will be kept.

> *For this reason I also suffer these things; nevertheless I am not ashamed, for I know whom I have believed and am persuaded that He is able to keep what I have committed to Him until that Day. 2Timothy 1:12*

God will keep everything that Paul entrusted to Him until the return of Jesus. Therefore, we are saved at all times until that day. If someday I went to hell it would not be a huge loss in the eyes of the world, but for the glory of God, the loss would mean a lot. This would damage His glory because it would mean that He had not kept me well. Because of His glory, we can say that there is no way to lose the salvation of God.

> *Now to Him who is able to keep you from stumbling, And to present you faultless before the presence of His glory with exceeding*

> *joy, To God our Savior, Who alone is wise, Be glory and majesty, Dominion and power, Both now and forever. Amen. Jude 1:24-25*

Since the Word of God states that the Lord is powerful to keep us from stumbling and falling, we can safely affirm that He does keep us. The big question is not if we are or are not capable of keeping our salvation. The question is if the Lord is capable of preserving our salvation. Scripture teaches that He is capable of preserving our salvation and He in fact does preserve it!

How does God keep us? He keeps us by hiding our lives together with Christ.

> *For you died, and your life is hidden with Christ in God. Colossians 3:3*

For us the life of God can only be lost if God Himself were to be lost. Thank God, He will never be lost. As a result, the life that He placed within us also will never be lost.

THE PROMISES OF GOD KEEP US.

Once you and I are saved by grace, no one can cast us out of God's hand, and so that we have assurance of this, God gave us promises that we would never be lost.

> *Most assuredly, I say to you, he who hears My word and believes in Him who sent Me has everlasting life, and shall not come into judgment, but has passed from death into life. John 5:24*

God is eternal and everything He does is for eternity. God would not save someone today, then turn around, and throw him or her in hell tomorrow. He will not save them again on the next day and then cast them in Hell again. If that were the case, the book of life would be full of eraser marks. God does not change His purposes for someone who becomes one of His children.

> *And I give them eternal life, and they shall never perish; neither shall anyone snatch them out of My hand. My Father, who has given them to Me, is greater than all; and no one is able to snatch them out of My Father's hand. I and My Father are one." John 10:28-30*

The Lord said, "No man is able to snatch them out of my Father's hand". In the original Greek, no man meant "no created thing". We are in the hands of God and no created thing can take us out of His hand. Thank God, nothing is greater than He is.

Some say: "The truth is that others can't pluck me out, but I myself can leave". Whoever says this is failing to consider all of the Word of God. If after a person receives salvation he could later lose it, could it be because he wanted to, that he no longer valued heaven and rather chose hell? Not even the sinner living in the world wants to go to hell. Not even Satan wishes to go to Hell! Those who act as if they do not care obviously do not have the slightest idea of what waits for them in Hell.

For a Christian to perish then, it must mean that the temptations of the world and the seduction of the enemy are able to deceive them and pluck them out of the hand of God. If demons and the world can do this, then we must conclude that they are more powerful than the Father of creation is. No my friend, not even you can jump out of the hand of God because you were included in the "no created thing" who could pluck them from the Father's hand referred to in John's epistle.

THE LOVE OF GOD KEEPS US.

Our Heavenly Father keeps our salvation for us; therefore, we can know that we are safe from eternal damnation now and always will be.

> *What then shall we say to these things? If God is for us, who can be against us? He who did not spare His own Son, but delivered Him up for us all, how shall He not with Him also freely give us all things? Who shall bring a charge against God's elect? It is God who justifies. Who is he who condemns? It is Christ who died, and furthermore is also risen, who is even at the right hand of God, who also makes intercession for us.*

> *Who shall separate us from the love of Christ? Shall tribulation, or distress, or persecution, or famine, or nakedness, or peril, or sword? As it is written: "For Your sake we are killed all day long; We are accounted as sheep for the slaughter." Yet in all these things we are more than conquerors through Him who loved us. For I am persuaded that neither death nor life, nor angels nor principalities nor powers, nor things present nor things to come, nor height nor depth, nor any other created thing, shall be able to*

*separate us from the love of God which is in Christ Jesus our
Lord. Romans 8:31-39*

Our salvation is not a matter of us loving the Lord, but of Him loving
us. Once He gave us His salvation, it is ours eternally. Nobody can
change or alter this fact. We are saved eternally.

SALVATION IS AN UNBREAKABLE COVENANT

Salvation is the last of a series of covenants that God has made with
man often called the "New Covenant". It is a blood covenant
completely conceived and developed by God. It is an agreement
between two parties so serious, that it can never be broken, only under
penalty of death. Through this agreement, all possessions and debts
become the property of both parties of the covenant.

Satan knows the power of covenants and that is why he demands their
use in his worship and rituals. The Hebrews celebrated covenants with
several symbols to affirm the terms of the covenant.

One of the symbols was that the two parties of the covenant exchanged
coats or outer clothing. This clothing symbolizes life, so the two parties
exchanged their lives for one another. Another symbol was the
exchange of belts, which symbolizes protection, or the idea that
whoever attacks one attacks the other and each would protect one
another.

Another part of the covenant ceremony was walking among the divided
blood sacrifice in a figure eight, which is a symbol of beginning a new
life together. In addition, those making the covenant would cut their
hand or wrist and mingle their blood one with the other to signify that
they were uniting as one.

They also ate bread and drank wine symbolizing that the life of one was
entering the body of the other. New names were also given to each to
signify that each had the right to the name of the other and finally trees
were planted and the terms of the covenant were carved into the trunks
symbolizing blessing in fulfilling the covenant and cursing for breaking
the covenant.

Marriage is an example of a blood covenant. The Word of God makes
it clear that the marriage covenant ends only with the death of either
the husband or the wife. "What God hath joined let no man separate"

are the words of our Lord.

God made a covenant with King David and established his throne forever. Jesus the son of David is the fulfillment of the covenant, which is an example of an eternal covenant. The new covenant is also an eternal covenant. This means that nothing can destroy it. No amount of sin, disobedience or unfaithfulness can make the covenant null or void.

Since salvation is a covenant, nothing can undo it. God established this covenant with man on the basis of His grace and He will see it through eternity on the basis of His grace. God does not base all His dealings with His people on grace, but He has based salvation through the new birth on grace from the beginning and lasting all throughout eternity. There is no end to salvation; it is by grace and it is eternal. Thank God for His unspeakable gift!

CHAPTER 3
THE KINGDOM FACTOR

THE KINGDOM OF HEAVEN: AN INTRODUCTION

In order to gain a correct understanding of what the bible calls "The gospel of the kingdom" it is important to understand some fundamental concepts. First, it is useful to know that only in the gospel of Matthew is the term "The gospel of the kingdom" used. No other part of the New Testament ever refers to the gospel as "The gospel of the kingdom". Mark refers to it one time as "the gospel of the kingdom of God." However, everywhere else the gospel writers used other names, the gospel of grace, the gospel of God, etc. It is also useful to recognize that the Gospel according to Matthew portrays Christ as king. It is a kingdom Gospel. The Gospel according to Mark portrays Christ as a servant, in Luke's account, as a true man, and in the Gospel of John, as God.

It is also significant that only in the gospel according to Matthew do we hear of the Kingdom of Heaven. Matthew used the term thirty-two times in his Gospel and the other New Testament writers zero times in the remaining books of the bible. What then does the Kingdom of Heaven mean? Can we say that the Kingdom of Heaven is the same as heaven? Can we say that the Kingdom of Heaven is the same as the Kingdom of God? For now, let me offer the following explanation and then I will gather scripture to explain what I believe the Holy Spirit has always intended that we understand by this distinction.

We can say that the difference between the Kingdom of Heaven and heaven is the difference between the rule of Christ on the earth during His Millennial Reign and the eternal state we call heaven. We can also affirm that the difference between the Kingdom of Heaven and the Kingdom of God is that the Kingdom of God extends all throughout eternity past present and future and the Kingdom of Heaven is that part of the Kingdom of God that will occur on the earth during Christ's millennial reign. In other words, the Kingdom of Heaven is to the Kingdom of God just as New York City is to the United States. Conversely, the Kingdom of God is not the Kingdom of Heaven just as the United States is not New York City. One is part of and contained in the other. This may sound trivial, but unless we understand this distinction, needless confusion will isolate us from the truth and weaken our conviction and effectiveness as Christians.

The reason I make a point of this is that if every time Christ speaks of the His millennial reign we understand that He is speaking of heaven we will understandably become confused. The two are part of completely different dispensations.

I always wondered why God would bother with the Millennium. Why not just get on with heaven and skip the Millennium? What exactly is the point of this one-thousand year-long prelude to heaven called the millennium? The answer to that question may have several aspects but I believe that at least one of them is that it is a time when God will distribute rewards and punishment to His people.

At this point, before we continue lets pause briefly on the subject of rewards. From time to time, I hear Christians make comments questioning the validity of expecting rewards, implying that the desire to receive rewards is somehow unspiritual. That sounds like a noble and religious attitude but I believe that in reality it is a notion derived from a worldly mind set. Sometimes Christians consider the desire for rewards as worldly or judge it as springing from impure motives and express their opposition of this desire with comments like "we should not be geared to expect rewards" and "we should do everything out of love without looking for reward".

In response to these arguments we should not neglect to recognize how God created us. What is it that moves us as human beings? What motivates us? By nature we are motivated by gaining, by winning, that is the point of sports and games. The spirit of the world seeks to rob us of our God given identity! God created us with the desire to receive recognition and love, to win, to advance. It is strange to expect someone to be motivated to lose, or to gain nothing for his or her efforts. Listen to the Apostle Paul in his epistle to the Philippians chapter 3:7-14

> *"But what things were gain to me, these I have counted loss for Christ. Yet indeed I also count all things loss for the excellence of the knowledge of Christ Jesus my Lord, for whom I have suffered the loss of all things, and count them as rubbish, that I may gain Christ and be found in Him, not having my own righteousness, which is from the law, but that which is through faith in Christ, the righteousness which is from God by faith; that I may know Him and the power of His resurrection, and the fellowship of His sufferings, being conformed to His death, if, by any means, I may attain to the resurrection from the dead.*
>
> *Not that I have already attained, or am already perfected; but I press on, that I may lay hold of that for which Christ Jesus has also laid hold of me. Brethren, I do not count myself to have apprehended; but one thing I do, forgetting those things which are behind and reaching forward to those things which are ahead, I press toward the goal for the prize of the upward call of God in Christ Jesus."*

Paul wanted the prize of the high calling of Christ, which is a reward. Why do people automatically think that the rewards that God refers to are limited to streets of gold and heavenly mansions? If God does in fact offer rewards then we should not think it improper to desire them. There is nothing spiritual about despising what God offers.

Just in one sermon alone from Matthew 5:12 to 6:18 Christ spoke of rewards at least nine times. The truth is that this whole section of Matthew's gospel deals with receiving rewards. Are we supposed to respond to Christ and say "no thanks I am not interested?" "No, I don't want your rewards?" "No, I am too spiritual for that?" As I indicated before, God's rewards are precious; we must not interpret them as mere trinkets. The crown of righteousness is not an object of gold placed on someone's head. The crown is a symbol of recognition to those believers who have responded as overcomers in this life.

Once we recognize that the crown is merely a symbol, we can begin to understand the utmost importance of the difference between salvation and reward. The reward is the recompense of the believer. What then is the difference between receiving salvation and receiving recompense? Salvation relates to and points to eternal life however; receiving recompense points to the time when the Lord distributes rewards to those of His servants who were faithful. We receive salvation by grace, through faith, and not by our works. The reward, on the other hand, depends on our merit.

Pastor Aluízio Silva my friend and mentor and the founder and leader of the Vine Church in Brazil shared an example that I believe helps immeasurably to understand the difference between salvation and reward. Let us suppose that I am a very wealthy man, the owner of a school, and you are a poor ignorant person, that wants to study and learn. So then, I offer to pay for your studies and for those of as many of your friends that wish to study with you. The registration and tuition are free as well as all the other educational expenses. That is what salvation is like. Jesus was very rich and He paid all the expenses necessary for you to study and attend private school. He paid for the registration, the tuition, everything! There is not detail that He has left unresolved for the furtherance of our education. Jesus has already paid the price for everything!

In spite of this, your diploma is not free. It is necessary for you to attend the classes and study, to take the tests and pass them. It would be absurd for us to think that the person who paid your expenses would also take your tests and study for you. No, you know that you would have to study hard and work up a sweat to pass the course. If you pass the final exam then you will be qualified to receive your diploma. The tuition was free, but the diploma comes at a great cost. Salvation is the tuition, by way of salvation (the new birth), all students are able to enter the school of God, but the diploma is the kingdom, the reward. Some Christians just want to remain in the school, because they like the fellowship and company of the students, the recesses, and the classes. However, all of this must result in good grades. Many enroll in the school, but not all receive a diploma. Many receive salvation, but not all will receive the recompense of the kingdom. Many are called, but few are chosen (Matthew 22:14).

Some people just want to be students for the rest of their lives. Instead of studying to prepare for a profession, they study just to study. There are many Christians like that today. They do not care if they graduate or not, they just study year after year. They do not want to develop a ministry they just want to study about the ministry and gain more and more knowledge about the bible and spiritual things.

Salvation is the paid tuition, the paid enrollment and expenses. Jesus has taken care of all the educational expenses, but now you must work and study ardently. This arduous work is the qualification necessary for receiving the diploma. In the end, you will take the test, and if you do not pass the test, you will not receive the diploma of a good and faithful servant.

No school principal will expel students from the school because they got a bad grade on a test. In the same way, nobody loses their salvation if they fail a test. What happens to students who do not do well on the test? They will have to repeat the school year or the course, or retake the test and maybe pay a fine. What will the millennium be then? The answer is the repetition of the course or school year. The problem is that it will last for a thousand years. It is a much better idea to make the effort and pass the test here!

We can only receive salvation through Christ. Only the blood of the Lamb can wash, forgive and justify us. The goal of sinners should be to receive salvation, but once we have already received salvation, our goal should be to receive the reward. Today we should be concerned about receiving the diploma at the end of the course.

If there is not clarity with respect to the difference between salvation and recompense, we will have a hard time understanding certain parts of the Bible. There are verses that speak with respect to reward but many people apply these to salvation. When they do this, they fall into error. That is why some people consider salvation as something so difficult and unattainable, that it would be easier to yield to all of the demands of religion. Salvation is in reality something very simple: it is enough just to believe with the heart and confess with the mouth that Jesus arose from the dead and is Lord (Romans 10:9-10). Receiving the reward on the other hand is not as simple.

THE CHRISTIAN AS AN OVERCOMER

"Yet in all these things we are more than conquerors through Him who loved us." (Romans 8:37)

If the reward is for the overcomers, then we could conclude that every Christian will receive a reward, because all are overcomers. This is true, but we need to understand the difference between legal and experimental position. Legally we as Christians are all more than conquerors. Christ guaranteed us the victory. However, it is possible for any Christian to fail to live this out in his experience. The legal position is that which we have in virtue of the new birth. In Christ Jesus, we are overcomers because He already paid the price; He died and rose again; He subjected principalities and powers. He overcame and because we are in Him, we have overcome as well. His position has become ours.

The experimental position, however, is to take into our experience that which is already legally ours. It is possible to be a legal heir of a great fortune, and, in practice, live in abject poverty. Some are sons of the King, but live as if they were slaves. I would even venture to say that most of God's children live as if they had no spiritual inheritance as princes and princesses, the titles given to children of royalty.

Charles Spurgeon tells of a poor elderly woman that he once went to pray for at her home. On a wall of her humble home was displayed a framed document which was given to her years earlier by someone that she used to work for as a house cleaner who was a member of British royalty.

It turned out to be a last will and testament worth millions of dollars but since the elderly woman did not know how to read or write she just thought it was a fancy and important looking document of no monetary value.

Spurgeon later informed her that she was legally a millionaire. She lived as a pauper all those years, legally very wealthy, but her experience was that of a poor elderly widow. How many Christians today are heirs of a spiritual fortune yet live as spiritual orphans destitute of God's riches?

Does that bother you? It pains me to think that we can be proprietors of a great fortune and live in poverty. This however is the life story of many Christians; they are legally rich, but experientially poor. God's part is to give, but our part is to receive, to appropriate. If there is no appropriation, there will be no enjoyment of the inheritance.

Overcomers are those who already have entered into the experience and have appropriated for themselves that which is every Christian's rightful inheritance. Therefore, there is a difference between being a saved child of God and being an overcomer.

Although every born again believer is legally an overcomer by right of spiritual inheritance, we know this is not the experience of all Christians. Many Christians live defeated lives. Is there such a thing as a defeated believer? Can a person who lives in spiritual defeated still be a born again believer? The answer is yes because our salvation and new birth is not only a question of experience but also of legality. Our salvation does not depend on our personal victory, but on the victory of the Lord Jesus. It is one thing to be a born again child of God, but it is another thing to be an overcomer. Salvation is the gift of God to those who believe in Him; but only the overcomer will experience the victory and receive the reward. Salvation comes by faith; however, the reward comes by works that we practice before God.

> *Now I say that the heir, as long as he is a child, does not differ at all from a slave, though he is master of all, (Galatians 4:1)*

Many Christians although they are sons of God, appear to be common slaves and it appears as though God treats them no differently than servants. They are "lords (masters) of all", but live as though they had nothing. The overcomers are all those believers that have already entered into the experience of the inheritance.

We should recognize that being an overcomer is a question of maturity. Overcomers are mature while defeated believers live like immature spiritual children. Overcomers are spiritual, while defeated Christians are carnal, immature and natural. Salvation is a matter of being in Christ, but the kingdom is a matter of Christ being in us, living His life within us and transmitting His character through us. We all have the legal victory over the devil; the flesh and the world, however not all possess the victory in their experience.

THE KINGDOM OF HEAVEN IS THE REWARD

The kingdom of Heaven is the period when the overcoming believers will receive their reward, this kingdom itself and its administration is the recompense or reward of those believers who enter into and grow in the experience of victory. In the Sermon on the Mount, in Matthew 5-7, the Lord speaks of the kingdom of heaven. The Lord's teachings tell us how a Christian can enter into the kingdom of heaven. Matthew repetitively speaks of rewards. The Lord Jesus mentioned the kingdom of heaven three times in the beatitudes.

> *Blessed are the poor in spirit, for theirs is the kingdom of heaven.*

> *Blessed are those who are persecuted for righteousness' sake, for theirs is the kingdom of heaven.*

> *Blessed are you when they revile and persecute you, and say all kinds of evil against you falsely for My sake. (Matthew 5:3, 10-12)*

We need to recognize that the kingdom of heaven itself is the reward. These promises show us that the privilege of administrating the kingdom together with Christ is the reward of God. There is no difference between the two. In the Sermon on the Mount, the Lord mentioned this matter many times, since He is talking about the kingdom.

> *For if you love those who love you, what reward have you? Do not even the tax collectors do the same? (Matthew 5:46)*

> *Take heed that you do not do your charitable deeds before men, to be seen by them. Otherwise, you have no reward from your Father in heaven. (Matthew 6:1)*

> *Therefore, when you do a charitable deed, do not sound a trumpet before you as the hypocrites do in the synagogues and in the streets, that they may have glory from men. Assuredly, I say to you, they have their reward. (Matthew 6:2)*

> *that your charitable deed may be in secret; and your Father who sees in secret will Himself reward you openly. (Matthew 6:4)*

> *But you, when you pray, go into your room, and when you have shut your door, pray to your Father who is in the secret place; and your Father who sees in secret will reward you openly. (Matthew 6:6)*

> *But you, when you fast, anoint your head and wash your face, so that you do not appear to men to be fasting, but to your Father who is in the secret place; and your Father who sees in secret will reward you openly. (Matthew 6:17, 18)*

The principal subject of the Sermon on the Mount is the kingdom of heaven. Jesus brought up the matter of reward in these three chapters several times because the kingdom of heaven is the reward.

"For the Son of Man will come in the glory of His Father with His angels, and then He will reward each according to his works. Assuredly, I say to you, there are some standing here who shall not taste death till they see the Son of Man coming in His kingdom."
(Matthew 16:27-28)

God will either reward or discipline a saved person according to his works. There are two factors here. First, each Christian will receive a reward according to his works, and second, Christ will distribute the reward when He comes in the glory of His Father with His angels. This will happen at the time when He returns to establish His kingdom on the Earth. Therefore, the Lord will not begin to distribute the rewards until the beginning of the kingdom of Heaven.

Then the seventh angel sounded: And there were loud voices in heaven, saying, "The kingdoms of this world have become the kingdoms of our Lord and of His Christ, and He shall reign forever and ever!" (Revelation 11:15)

The nations were angry, and Your wrath has come, And the time of the dead, that they should be judged, And that You should reward Your servants the prophets and the saints, And those who fear Your name, small and great, And should destroy those who destroy the earth. (Revelation 11:18)

When the Lord becomes the King and the kingdoms of the world becomes the kingdom of our Lord and of His Christ, then that will be the time for giving the rewards to the saints, to the small and great. In other words, the time of the kingdom is the time of reward. When the kingdom comes, the reward will come also.

The reward will be the receiving of the crown and the throne. What is a crown? It is not merely a sculptured piece of gold with diamond insets to wear on the head. A crown is a symbol. The crown represents a position in the kingdom and the glory of the kingdom. When a ruler loses his crown, he loses power that it represents. The crown and the throne are symbols of the kingdom.

For what is our hope, or joy, or crown of rejoicing? Is it not even you in the presence of our Lord Jesus Christ at His coming? (1Thess. 2:19)

Paul said:

> *"Finally, there is laid up for me the crown of righteousness, which the Lord, the righteous Judge, will give to me on that Day, and not to me only but also to all who have loved His appearing." (2Timothy 4:8)*

Paul was not looking to receive anything to put on his head. He knew that the crown was a position in the kingdom. To receive it, it is necessary that the believer receive God's approval.

> *Blessed is the man who endures temptation; for when he has been approved, he will receive the crown of life which the Lord has promised to those who love Him. (James 1:12)*

> *. . . and when the Chief Shepherd appears, you will receive the crown of glory that does not fade away. (1Peter 5:4)*

Jesus warned the members of the Church in Philadelphia against the risk of losing their crown.

> *Behold, I am coming quickly! Hold fast what you have, that no one may take your crown. (Revelation 3:11)*

Just as the crown is a reward, the throne is also a reward for the overcomer. The throne is not just a golden chair. It is also a symbol of the kingdom representing position, authority and glory in the kingdom. When we hear that a king of some country loses the throne, in reality he lost his kingdom. The throne and the crown as objects are not significant; they only exist to symbolize the kingdom. The bible clearly shows us that the reward is simply the privileges of the kingdom. .

CHAPTER 4

SALVATION AND THE KINGDOM

The kingdom will not only be the time when the overcoming believers receive their reward, the kingdom itself is the reward! There is a fundamental need to understand the difference between receiving salvation and receiving the recompense of the kingdom. Many Christians are content with salvation and an entrance to heaven, but salvation is just the front door to the kingdom, once we pass through the door, the Lord wants us to progress until we receive the kingdom. Let us see how the Word of God makes a distinction between Salvation and the Kingdom of Heaven.

SALVATION IS RECEIVED BY GRACE THROUGH FAITH; THE KINGDOM IS RECEIVED BY WORKS

Salvation is a gift. The Word of God never teaches that we can receive it by works. Nobody can buy salvation, Jesus already paid for it. He bought and paid for it so that nobody else can buy what He has already purchased and paid for. We need to be firm concerning the fact that salvation is by grace and nothing else! Salvation will not come with the confession of the name of the Lord plus deliverance, or confession accompanied with the attitude of giving up smoking, or changing your style of clothes, or any other way. Salvation is a gift that comes to us by grace, through faith. It is by grace and only by grace.

The true invitation of the Lord is "Come as you are, but come!" He does not tell anyone to "first purify yourself", or "first change your habits". The Lord will change your life. This is the gospel of grace: our salvation.

> *"Ho! Everyone who thirsts, Come to the waters; And you who have no money, Come, buy and eat. Yes, come, buy wine and milk Without money and without price. (Isaiah 55:1)*

> *And the Spirit and the bride say, "Come!" And let him who hears say, "Come!" And let him who thirsts come. Whoever desires, let him take the water of life freely. (Revelation 22:17)*

> *For the wages of sin is death, but the gift of God is eternal life in Christ Jesus our Lord. (Rom. 6:23)*

A gift is the same as a present. Salvation is a gift given to us with no strings attached. The only condition is that we believe. If we believe, then we will be saved.

> *For by grace you have been saved through faith, and that not of yourselves; it is the gift of God, not of works, lest anyone should boast. (Eph. 2:8, 9)*

I know that it is hard to believe that it could be that simple, but here we have it in black and white. We cannot honestly interpret it any other way. Either Salvation is free, or it has a price that we must pay for it. It did have a price, a high price, but Jesus paid it all!

Salvation happens in an instant. God regenerates our human spirit when we receive eternal life within us. Salvation is the door, through which we enter.

> *. . . that if you confess with your mouth the Lord Jesus and believe in your heart that God has raised Him from the dead, you will be saved. For with the heart one believes unto righteousness, and with the mouth confession is made unto salvation. (Romans 10:9, 10)*

Salvation deals with the problem of Hell, but becoming an overcomer points to the matter of reward. Many Christians are only concerned about escaping Hell, but once we receive salvation, we should forget the matter of Hell because we have not only received salvation we have become God's begotten children.

> *"But as many as received Him, to them He gave the right to become children of God, to those who believe in His name:" (John 1:12)*

I have two sons, and no matter how many bad things they may do, they will never cease to be my sons. The Lord also states that no one plucks any of those who come to Him out of His hand. (John 10:28) I understand that not all believe in this way. Arminianism and Calvinism are the two theological lines of thought that debate whether salvation can be lost or not. The Arminian position teaches that salvation depends on us and that, if we are faithful until the end, we will be saved. The Calvinist, however, preaches that salvation does not depend on us but that it is a gift of God. If I receive it, then God will never take it back. Apparently, these two views appear to contradict one another, but there can be an equilibrium between the two.

Both lines of thought have scriptural backing, but, even so, both cause some problems. Generally the Armenian considers only the aspect of salvation, the Armenian almost never considers the matter of reward; normally, the Armenian will teach that, if you come to Jesus, you will receive a reward in heaven. Such teaching is incorrect however; Scripture has never taught that anyone will receive a reward for receiving Jesus as Savior. It is incorrect to interpret salvation as a reward. Salvation is one thing and reward is something distinctly separate.

The Arminians are mistaken on this point. Many Arminians live in constant fear, because each time that they fall into sin they conclude that they are in danger of losing their salvation. I am speaking in general terms, because not all Christians of the Armenian persuasion think this way. Generally, however the Armenian position makes for a more zealous and committed believer because of the fear of being lost if not sufficiently faithful.

For the Calvinists however, there is no loss of salvation. They generally place more weight on God's sovereignty than on man's responsibility. Since for them there is no loss of salvation, many end up living lax spiritual lives. Since God is sovereign, they conclude that it is not necessary to pray, fast or serve the Lord with zeal. Many Calvinists become third rate Christians. They are believers, they have spiritual life, but in general, they do not live as overcomers. They think that because salvation is something that only God operates in the Christian that everything else in the Christian life is also exclusively His doing. However, scripture refutes this many times. We see examples in the Old Testament where God commanded men to do things and then turned around and said that He did them. It is because He works through the works of man. The New Testament teaches us that we are co-laborers together with Him.

I am seeking to emphasize the balance between the vision of grace and of works. On one hand, you are saved by grace, on the other; you are saved for good works. Thus, you will no longer be judged with respect to salvation; however, with respect to reward, you will be judged and deemed worthy on the basis of having practiced good works that deserve the approval of God or not.

The Calvinist position is useful because it teaches the truth that salvation is by grace. A gift cannot be lost. While the Arminianism position is useful because it preaches commitment, seriousness with respect to God's commands and watching and praying, even if all this is for fear of going to Hell. We can harmonize these two lines of theology. We need to balance the two. Salvation is by grace through faith, while the kingdom depends on works subsequent to having received salvation. Some preachers and teachers say that, if you come to Jesus, you will receive a crown in Heaven. This is definitely contrary to the Word of God. Nobody will receive a crown just because he or she has received salvation. It is necessary to have works. We receive salvation by faith and only by faith but for the works. Jesus said:

> *". . . and all the churches shall know that I am He who searches the minds and hearts. And I will give to each one of you according to your works." (Revelation 2:23)*

If we receive salvation entirely by grace through faith, how do we receive the kingdom? The answer is by fulfilling the conditions of God connected to faithfulness, holiness, and perseverance. Jesus said in the Sermon on the Mount:

> *"Blessed are the poor in spirit, for theirs is the kingdom of heaven." (Matthew 5:3)*

Is it necessary to be poor in spirit to enter Heaven? We have already shown that salvation is by grace therefore we do not need any special virtues to receive salvation. Do you believe sinners possess any spiritual virtues? All sinners are miserable, arrogant and proud, as are many Christians unfortunately. However, if the sinner believes with his heart and confesses with his mouth, he will be saved. On the other hand, Jesus said, to inherit the kingdom, it is necessary to be poor in spirit and deny yourself.

In the same way, it is not necessary to suffer persecution in order to receive salvation. However, to receive the reward of reining with the Lord, there will be times when you will need to endure persecution because of righteousness, because Jesus said:

> *Blessed are those who are persecuted for righteousness' sake, For theirs is the kingdom of heaven. (Matthew 5:10)*

> *For I say to you, that unless your righteousness exceeds the righteousness of the scribes and Pharisees, you will by no means enter the kingdom of heaven. (Matthew 5:20)*

If you think that in order to receive salvation you need to be holier than the Pharisees were, then you have serious problems! Probably, very few of us would make it to heaven if this were true. From an external viewpoint, the Pharisees were blameless. Imagine someone who was so correct that they tithed on some mint or other kind of spice that someone handed to them. If someone gives you a stick of gum, do you tear off a tenth part to give back as a tithe? Careful, if you believe that the beatitudes are speaking of salvation you could go to hell for such an oversight! However to inherit the kingdom and be an overcomer, your righteousness must greatly exceed that of the Pharisees.

> *"Not everyone who says to Me, 'Lord, Lord,' shall enter the kingdom of heaven, but he who does the will of My Father in heaven. (Matthew 7:21)*

To receive salvation, you don't have to first do the will of God, rather you must confess with your mouth and believe in your heart as Romans 10:9 says. However to reign, we must do His will. How many Christians can honestly say that they are faithful in doing God's will? We must recognize that there are Christians who have received salvation yet do not practice God's will. However, such Christians cannot say that they are overcomers.

> *"And from the days of John the Baptist until now the kingdom of heaven suffers violence, and the violent take it by force." (Matthew 11:12)*

It is not necessary to be violent, to fight and scratch to receive your salvation because it is a gift of grace. However, the people of God can only receive the kingdom by works, and frequently, the works require force and strength and a resolute perseverance that can be called violence. The Word of God, repetitively, shows us each Christian receives his rewarded according to his works.

> *"And behold, I am coming quickly, and My reward is with Me, to give to every one according to his work." (Revelation 22:12)*

> *"Now he who plants and he who waters are one, and each one will receive his own reward according to his own labor." (1 Corinthians 3:8)*

> *"And whatever you do, do it heartily, as to the Lord and not to men, knowing that from the Lord you will receive the reward of the inheritance; for you serve the Lord Christ" (Colossians 3:23-24)*

> *"Now to him who works, the wages are not counted as grace but as debt." (Romans 4:4)*

SALVATION IS ETERNAL WHILE THE DURATION OF THE KINGDOM WILL BE ONE THOUSAND YEARS

Salvation will not last longer for some than for others it is equally eternal for everyone. However, the kingdom of heaven will last during the one thousand years of the Millennium when some will reign and others will suffer discipline. The kingdom has a beginning and ending; salvation has no end.

> *Then comes the end, when He delivers the kingdom to God the Father, when He puts an end to all rule and all authority and power. For He must reign till He has put all enemies under His feet. (1 Corinthians 15:24-25)*

SALVATION DOES NOT REQUIRE ANY SACRIFICE BEYOND THAT WHICH CHRIST ALREADY SUFFERED ON THE CROSS, BUT THE KINGDOM REQUIRES SACRIFICE AND SOMETIMES SUFFERING

Salvation does not require anyone to live in poverty. No Christian really believes that in order to receive salvation he must sell all his material possessions, but Jesus said:

> *"And again I say to you, it is easier for a camel to go through the eye of a needle than for a rich man to enter the kingdom of God"*

(Matthew 19:24).

During the last few decades, many rich and famous people have come into the church but never has anyone said, finally, the camel went through the eye of the needle. Salvation is a gift. It is not necessary to give or donate anything whatsoever to receive salvation.

However, the kingdom is different. If as a saved and born again child of God, I still manifest an attitude of greed and love of money, I would be acting like a defeated Christian and I will disqualify myself from receiving any reward. It is quite difficult for a rich person to become an overcomer, because of the great love that the rich have devoted to money. It is rare to find a rich man who is completely faithful in paying his tithe. They give great amounts that do not even correspond to a tenth of a tenth of their income, much less the surpassing righteousness demanded to inherit the kingdom.

Jesus taught:

> *"For there are eunuchs who were born thus from their mother's womb, and there are eunuchs who were made eunuchs by men, and there are eunuchs who have made themselves eunuchs for the kingdom of heaven's sake. He who is able to accept it, let him accept it." Matt.19:12*

Salvation does not depend on one's marital status nor is it necessary to make a vow of chastity, however to receive the reward, sometimes this is necessary. For example, if you have never married, you should remain sexually pure until the day that you get married. Otherwise, if you live in sexual impurity you will be a defeated Christian.

Revelation 20 shows us that the martyrs will receive the kingdom although it does not say that they will be the only ones who receive it (see verse 4). The Bible, however, never teaches that a man must become a martyr in order to receive eternal life. The kingdom, however, is different. In the kingdom, God demands that we put forth an effort, including possible martyrdom to receive it.

> *And I saw thrones, and they sat on them, and judgment was committed to them. Then I saw the souls of those who had been beheaded for their witness to Jesus and for the word of God, who had not worshiped the beast or his image, and had not received his*

mark on their foreheads or on their hands. And they lived and reigned with Christ for a thousand years. (Revelation 20:4)

SALVATION IS A GIFT BUT THE KINGDOM IS A CONQUEST

On one occasion, the mother of James and John approached Jesus with a special request, and said:

"And He said to her, "What do you wish?" She said to Him, "Grant that these two sons of mine may sit, one on Your right hand and the other on the left, in Your kingdom." But Jesus answered and said, "You do not know what you ask. Are you able to drink the cup that I am about to drink, and be baptized with the baptism that I am baptized with?" They said to Him, "We are able." So He said to them, "You will indeed drink My cup, and be baptized with the baptism that I am baptized with; but to sit on My right hand and on My left is not Mine to give, but it is for those for whom it is prepared by My Father." (Matthew 20:21-23)

The Lord did not grant this mother's request because the kingdom is not something that is given as a gift or favor, it is something that is rewarded by works and performance. The kingdom is a reward earned by merit. The two brothers even told the Lord that they would drink the cup; however, even so, He did not grant them their request.

At the cross, just before death, one of the thieves crucified with Christ made the same request:

"Then he said to Jesus, "Lord, remember me when You come into Your kingdom." And Jesus said to him, "Assuredly, I say to you, today you will be with Me in Paradise." (Luke 23:42-43)

The thief made a request concerning his status in the kingdom, but Jesus answered concerning his salvation. Concerning the kingdom, there was nothing more that he could have done at that point. He had no chance to practice any works of righteousness since he waited until the time of his death to be born again. He had no time to practice any works for which he could have received a reward. It was as if Jesus had said, "Today you will be saved, but as far as the kingdom is concerned, nothing more can be done, it is too late.

Many people in the church today are deceived concerning what happens at death. They somehow imagine that death has the power to perfect them. The truth is that if we die ignorant of spiritual things here, we will be ignorant of spiritual things when God resurrects us there. If we die without having practiced deeds of righteousness here, we will arrive there with no works. In other words, death does not change our spiritual status.

> *"Blessed are the dead who die in the Lord from now on." "Yes,"*
> *says the Spirit, "that they may rest from their labors, and their*
> *works follow them." (Revelation 14:13)*

If the works of those who have labored in the kingdom will follow them in death, it is only logical to conclude that those who have no works here will have no works to follow them there.

Death has no power to add anything to us. Those who die as children in the faith here will arrive as children in the faith there. No one will acquire knowledge in the blink of an eye just by leaving their mortal bodies behind and taking on a glorified spiritual body. Nobody will suddenly, acquire works before the Lord just because they died when they had no opportunity, or didn't take advantage of the opportunities that they had to work while they were still here. If death had the power to add something to us or to transform us, the Lord would not have had to die on the cross.

The Millennium will be the time that Christ will complete the work that He began in the life of many Christians. He will fulfill His promise. We know that many people die without having completed the work that God has entrusted to them.

> *"being confident of this very thing, that He who has begun a good*
> *work in you will complete it until the day of Jesus Christ."*
> *(Philippians 1:6)*

The Day of Jesus Christ comes at the end of the Millennium at the battle of Armageddon when the Lord takes vengeance over His enemies.

The Lord looks for fruit, as we see in the passage of the true Vine in John chapter 15. Jesus stated clearly:

> *"I am the vine, you are the branches. He who abides in Me, and I*
> *in him, bears much fruit; for without Me you can do nothing. If*
> *anyone does not abide in Me, he is cast out as a branch and is*

withered; and they gather them and throw them into the fire, and they are burned." Jn. 15:5, 6

Whoever bears no fruit in this life, will pass through the fire of God's discipline during the Millennium. If we sin here on earth and go into the Millennium in sin, we will appear before the Lord in the same way. If there is any unrepentant sin in the life of a Christian in this age, there will be discipline in the next age and possibly even in this present age.

The Lord said:

> *"Agree with your adversary quickly, while you are on the way with him, lest your adversary deliver you to the judge, the judge hand you over to the officer, and you be thrown into prison..." (Matthew 5:25)*

This exhortation affirms that we must settle accounts with those who have legitimate grievances against us. If we delay, the other party may die then there will be no way to correct the problem, he will take the matter up with the judge. "The way", in this text, refers to while we are still alive here on earth. If you die with any unresolved matter, on judgment day, the Lord will demand an accounting and consequently, He may mete out discipline and punishment. Make no mistake thinking that death will free you from the discipline of the Lord. The Father disciplines His children at any time He wishes.

However, this matter is not limited only to offenses committed against others; we also need to be careful to hold no grudges against others. Jesus said that if we do not forgive those who offend us or who are our debtors in this age, He would deliver us to the tormentors in that day.

> *"And his master was angry, and delivered him to the torturers until he should pay all that was due to him. So My heavenly Father also will do to you if each of you, from his heart, does not forgive his brother his trespasses." (Matthew 18:34-35)*

Eternal life is equal for all, but in the kingdom, there will be different levels of reward and position among believers.

Each person will receive a reward according to his works. Whoever has no works, will receive no reward. Whoever has practiced evil works will suffer correction and discipline. In the kingdom, there are different levels of responsibility, authority and reward. Some will receive ten cities, others five.

> *"And he said to him, 'Well done, good servant; because you were faithful in a very little, have authority over ten cities.' And the second came, saying, 'Master, your mina has earned five minas.' Likewise he said to him, 'You also be over five cities.''' (Luke 19:17-19)*

Some servants will receive a reward; others however will not. Some will receive a rich entrance into the kingdom and some will enter without such an honor.

> *". . . for so an entrance will be supplied to you abundantly into the everlasting kingdom of our Lord and Savior Jesus Christ."* (2Peter 1:11)

While there will be varying levels during the kingdom age, in the eternal state of heaven there will be no levels, everyone will receive equal treatment. No one will receive ten more or less of anything in heaven, but this will be the case during the millennial reign of Christ.

The kingdom and eternal life are two distinct things. The condition for salvation is faith in the Lord. Beyond faith, there is no other condition, because Jesus Christ fulfilled all the requirements for our salvation. The death of His Son satisfied all the demands of God's righteousness. However, entering into the kingdom of heaven is another matter; works are required. Today man is saved by the justice of God, however we can't enter into the kingdom of Heaven unless our righteousness is far superior to that of the scrupulous Pharisees and scribes (Matthew 5:20) Salvation is a matter of knowing the Lord, but the kingdom is a matter of us being known by Him.

The matter of eternal life has as its only basis the work of the Lord Jesus Christ. However, the matter of the kingdom also depends on the works of God's children. Of course, God's children do the works in dependence on the power of God, but the point is that God's people must do them.

Even the kingdom, is in the end, a matter of grace. After all, what works could we do for God in our own strength? So if we do them in His strength, how can we not marvel that even so, He rewards us? The bible teaches that God is not served by human hands, but even so we are called to be His servants and "workers together with Him" (Acts 7:25; 1Cor. 3:9). It is a privilege for us when God calls us His helpers. Just think about it, what work could we possibly do at a level of sufficient excellency to be able to please the divine pattern of Him who created the heavens and the earth? Only by grace, can this happen.

What about those who convert at an old age with little time to produce good works before God and store up treasures in heaven, how will God treat them? Even if someone converts later, at an older age, he may have a reward equal to that of those who have converted at a young age and had more time to accumulate heavenly treasures, because God looks principally at the intent of the heart. We can see this principle in the parable of the workers in the vineyard in Matthew 20:

> *"So when evening had come, the owner of the vineyard said to his steward, 'Call the laborers and give them their wages, beginning with the last to the first.' And when those came who were hired about the eleventh hour, they each received a denarius. But when the first came, they supposed that they would receive more; and they likewise received each a denarius. And when they had received it, they complained against the landowner, saying, 'These last men have worked only one hour, and you made them equal to us who have borne the burden and the heat of the day.'*
>
> *But he answered one of them and said, 'Friend, I am doing you no wrong. Did you not agree with me for a denarius? Take what is yours and go your way. I wish to give to this last man the same as to you. Is it not lawful for me to do what I wish with my own things? Or is your eye evil because I am good?' So the last will be first, and the first last. For many are called, but few chosen"* (Matt. 20:8-16).

AT THE NEW BIRTH, ETERNAL LIFE HAS ALREADY BEEN DETERMINED, BUT THE REWARD AND RECOMPENSE ARE MATTERS NOT YET DECIDED

God has already determined the eternal life of every Christian; therefore, we can be sure of our salvation. However, the reward is something that He has not yet determined. Reward depends on if we participate in the race or not and how we finish it. It is possible to be an overcomer today and tomorrow no longer be and vice versa. Solomon is a good example of someone who started well and ended badly. Jacob was the opposite; he began badly and ended well. The reward therefore is something that God will yet decide and the person who has qualified to receive a crown today may not be qualified tomorrow.

"Behold, I am coming quickly! Hold fast what you have, that no one may take your crown." (Revelation 3:11)

Again, it is necessary to point out the differences between salvation and reward. We receive salvation by faith; we receive our reward by works. Salvation is eternal; the reward lasts a thousand years. Salvation never depends on human merit but on the grace of God. On the other hand, the reward is not a gift, but something earned by good works.

Jesus told several "kingdom parables" in the Gospel of Matthew to illustrate the principle I have just outlined. One of these is the Parable of the Talents. In Matthew 25:14-30 Jesus taught His disciples that one day all of His servants would give an accounting of what they have done with their lives.

"For the kingdom of heaven is like a man traveling to a far country, who called his own servants and delivered his goods to them. And to one he gave five talents, to another two, and to another one, to each according to his own ability; and immediately he went on a journey.

Then he who had received the five talents went and traded with them, and made another five talents. And likewise he who had received two gained two more also. But he who had received one went and dug in the ground, and hid his lord's money.

After a long time the lord of those servants came and settled accounts with them. So he who had received five talents came and brought five other talents, saying, 'Lord, you delivered to me five talents; look, I have gained five more talents besides them.' His lord said to him, 'Well done, good and faithful servant; you were faithful over a few things, I will make you ruler over many things. Enter into the joy of your lord.' He also who had received two talents came and said, 'Lord, you delivered to me two talents; look, I have gained two more talents besides them.' His lord said to him, 'Well done, good and faithful servant; you have been faithful over a few things, I will make you ruler over many things. Enter into the joy of your lord.'

Then he who had received the one talent came and said, 'Lord, I knew you to be a hard man, reaping where you have not sown, and gathering where you have not scattered seed. And I was afraid, and went and hid your talent in the ground. Look, there you have what is yours.' But his lord answered and said to him, 'You wicked and lazy servant, you knew that I reap where I have not sown, and gather where I have not scattered seed. So you ought to have deposited my money with the bankers, and at my coming I would have received back my own with interest. Therefore take the talent from him, and give it to him who has ten talents. For to everyone who has, more will be given, and he will have abundance; but from him who does not have, even what he has will be taken away. And cast the unprofitable servant into the outer darkness. There will be weeping and gnashing of teeth."

Jesus first directed this parable to the twelve disciples therefore; it applies to all Christians: to those who know the Lord. After reading verse 30, which describes the "wicked and slothful servant" that will be cast into the outer darkness where there will be, weeping and gnashing of teeth, most people conclude that this parable is talking about the unsaved. This however cannot be so. This parable, like all the kingdom parables is for the children of God, for the servants of God.

The word translated "servant" in English means slave in the original Greek, someone who was purchased. God did not hire us as employees He purchased us. He bought us with the high price of the blood of the Lord Jesus Christ. Thus, we are slaves. We have an owner; we belong to the one who bought us. We belong to the Lord who bought and sealed us with His mark of ownership.

There are two types of slaves described in the Bible. The truth is that the Lord bought us so that He could make us free. In the Old Testament, there is a law that deals with slaves. This law taught that no one could buy and own a slave for more than 50 years. Every fifty years the Jewish people celebrated the Year of Jubilee and they called every seventh year the "Sabbath year". Nobody could be a slave for his or her whole life.

Whenever one of these special years occurred, there was a general declaration of freedom. The law also determined that if a specific slaved did not wish to leave his owner, even to gain his own freedom, but rather learned to love his master and desired to remain as a slave he should receive a mark: he could have his ear pierced by an awl. From that day on, he would remain a slave for the rest of his life to that owner, and could never again claim his freedom. His destiny would be to serve his master for the rest of his life.

We are like this slave. One day the Lord freed us, giving us a deed of freedom, erasing with His precious blood the note of debt that weighed against us (Colossians 2:14). Then He told us "Now you are free, you can go." However, we have nowhere to go; only He has the words of eternal life. We do not want to leave; we only want to stay with Him.

In Ephesians 1:13 we learn that God sealed His children with the Holy Spirit of promise. In Bible times, kings used rings on their fingers as seals stamping their impression on hot wax thus sealing royal documents. The church is the flock of God and as His property; we have His mark showing that we are His exclusive property. When Satan sees the flock of God, he can try to destroy it. However, there is one thing that he cannot do: he cannot rob it. Because once we have been sealed, there is no one who is able to pluck us out of the hand of the Father (John 10:28). We are then slaves who voluntarily desire to serve the Lord because we love Him.

The parable of the ten virgins emphasizes watching and praying, and being filled with the Holy Spirit; it deals with the affectionate relationship between a bride and groom. In the parable of the Talents however, the emphasis is different, it deals with our faithfulness in relation to the gifts of the Holy Spirit and how we use and multiply what the Lord entrusted to us as His servants and His slaves. While the parable of the virgins points to the rapture, the parable of the Talents refers to the Judgment Seat of Christ.

If is of fundamental importance in order to understand this parable that we recognize that we possess a double relationship with God. On one hand, we are sons. We are God's children, begotten of His seed. We are part of the family of God. Therefore, we are heirs of the Lord, and joint heirs with Christ. We are co-heirs with Jesus, since we are also sons of God.

On the other hand, we are servants. In relation to God the Father, we are sons, but in relation to the Lord Jesus, we are servants. With God the Father, our relationship is based on grace, but with the Lord Jesus Christ, our relationship is based on works and responsibility.

In order to avoid confusion in reading and studying the Word of God, it is important to understand these two aspects, and to know what type of relationship each portion of scripture is dealing with in each situation. There are scriptures that speak of the relationship of grace;

but in others, we see the need for being responsible, since God told us that one day, we will have to give an accounting of our works and deeds. In the Parable of the Talents, we find an example of a portion of scripture that deals with responsibility.

Grace will neither reward nor recompense anyone, just as works will save no one. Each one has its place. The reward is for the one who faithfully uses what he has received and multiplies what is in his responsibility. Salvation is granted to all those who believe with the heart and confess Jesus as Lord with the mouth. It is by grace that we are saved; however, it is by works that we will be rewarded.

THE LORD DISTRIBUTES HIS TALENTS (GOODS)

"For the kingdom of heaven is like a man traveling to a far country, who called his own servants and delivered his goods to them. And to one he gave five talents, to another two, and to another one, to each according to his own ability; and immediately he went on a journey." Matthew 25:14, 15

The man in this parable, who traveled to a far country, is undisputedly the Lord Jesus Christ. The far country is the heavenly realm, and the country that he left behind is the world. The Lord dwelt among us physically in flesh and blood and today He does so in the spiritual realm through the Holy Spirit. He was present with us and then traveled to a far country. This trip refers to His ascension after the resurrection.

Before he left, he called together his own servants. Some bible teachers affirm that these servants refer to the Jews. This is not a correct interpretation however because in the New Testament slaves and servants are those who have been bought with a price. The Jews as a people have never recognized Jesus as their Messiah. The Jewish prophets, kings and priests were the servants of God under the Old Testament but not in the New Testament.

The Lord possesses goods and these He delivers to His own servants. The Lord only delivered the goods that He possesses to His servants. Why would He entrust His goods to the ungodly: to those who mock His name, and do not do what He commands or desires? No, the Lord only entrusts His goods to His own servants, to those who have been born again, to His Church. The unsaved, the ungodly are not God's servants; they belong to Satan and are servants of Satan and sin. This parable therefore is for and concerning God's New Testament people: the Church.

So then, what goods was Jesus referring to in this parable? What does the Lord have that He has delivered to us? I believe that the answer is the ministry of discipleship or the spiritual care of souls. Verse 15 tells us that the Lord gave talents to His servants. What exactly is a talent? A commonly mistaken interpretation is that the talents refer to possessions, position, education, intelligence, diplomas and status. In the Word of God a talent does not represent these things. God allows any person to possess these things. Even the ungodly have all these things, and quite often in greater quantities than Christians. Talents do not refer to natural things. Talents are the possessions of the Lord. They are the privileges and responsibilities of the spiritual care of His people.

In this parable, the Lord gave five talents to one servant, two talents to another and one talent to a third: each one according to his ability (vs.15). From what Jesus mentioned in this parable, we can arrive at several practical conclusions.

A talent is something that only believers can receive, because the talents are the goods that the Lord left for His servants, those who have been born again. God does not give these talents indiscriminately, but according to the ability of each servant. You may wonder how God determines the ability of each servant. While this is an honest question, within the text there appears to be no answer. I suppose that one's ability would depend on several varying factors but one thing we can be sure of: God is a just God and depending upon our response will reward us accordingly. In any case, the text of the parable implies that God considers the ability of each servant and bestowed talents to each one based on their ability to use them properly. The ability is not the talent; rather it is that which helps us use the talent. However, each servant must accept the responsibility and eventually give account of the multiplication of their talents. In any case, God determines the ability, gives the proper amount of talents, and expects a return on His investment.

We can also observe that God may increase the amount of talents that He originally gives when His servants are faithful in using and multiplying them. The servant, who received five talents, gained five more, the one who received two, gained two more. So if any given servant is faithful in multiplying what he has been given he can hope to receive more, or in other words no servant is given a fixed amount of talents. God gives each servant an initial amount and from then on, it depends on his faithfulness in multiplying what God has given him. The Word clearly demonstrates that each servant should develop his talents and that the talents speak of spiritual things since they are the Lord's goods bestowed upon His own servants.

God can recall the talents. The parable goes on to explain that the servant who received one talent buried it, and in the end the Lord took it back and gave it to the one that had ten. Here again we can see that the talents are not natural abilities since once a person learns something they cannot suddenly loose what they have learned. For example if I learn to play the guitar, I can't all of the sudden lose that ability because I was somehow unfaithful in multiplying it, even less so could that ability be automatically transferred to someone else who was more faithful with their specific talent.

In this parable, the master took the talent back. Therefore, these talents are not natural but spiritual. One day at the Judgment Seat of Christ, the Lord will require an accounting of our use of His goods (talents). If we have not multiplied these talents, we will have to give an account at the Judgment Seat of Christ and subsequently disciplined. Those servants whom God deems faithful will receive even more talents as reward from the Lord.

> *For whoever has, to him more will be given, and he will have abundance; but whoever does not have, even what he has will be taken away from him. (Matthew 13:12)*

> *Therefore take the talent from him, and give it to him who has ten talents. (Matthew 25:28)*

All servants receive talents. These three servants represent all the servants of God. Some receive more, some receive less, some are faithful and some are unfaithful.

It is also important to note how the servants "traded" with the talents they had received.

> *Then he who had received the five talents went and traded with them, and made another five talents. And likewise he who had received two gained two more also. (Matthew 25:16-17)*

The Lord distributed His talents. The servants, who received five and two talents respectively, right away went out and "traded" with them. Notice that the Lord did not command them to go out and trade with their talents . . . they went out voluntarily. How is it that they knew they should act in this manner? The answer is that they perceived the intention of their Lord. They understood the mind of their Lord. Therefore, they went out and negotiated with their talents.

To know the mind of the Lord is something fundamental for all those who want to fulfill the purpose of God and be qualified as overcomers. To know the Lord is something very serious. Verse 18 says that the servant that had received one talent dug a hole and hid his talent. The servant hid his talent because he did not know the Lord.

> *Then he who had received the one talent came and said, 'Lord, I knew you to be a hard man, reaping where you have not sown, and gathering where you have not scattered seed. And I was afraid, and went and hid your talent in the ground. Look, there you have what is yours.' (Matthew 25:24-25)*

What? He was afraid of the Lord? Could that be right? Could it be that we should fear the Lord in this way? Is it correct to say that the Lord reaps where He has not sown, or gathers where He has not strewn? Who is like that? Nobody can expect to reap where he has not sown! God is nothing like what this servant had accused Him of being. This servant had a twisted concept of who his Lord was. He thought that his Lord was a severe and unjust authoritarian despot. Nowhere in scripture is God described in this manner. On the contrary He is a gracious, patient and generous giver who has bestowed upon us, everything that we have. We have nothing that He has not granted us, or allowed us to possess.

The first two servants negotiated with their talents and turned a profit, multiplying them, without someone commanding them to do so. They did this because they had discerned the mind of their Lord. The one that buried his talent did so because he was afraid. He was afraid because he did not sufficiently know his Lord. A proper vision of God is vital to our spiritual growth.

What is your vision of God? Your vision of God depends on where you received it. Many Christians have received a very flawed and distorted view of God. If each child of God would spend time in meditation on the Word of God, the truth could correct these flawed concepts. Unfortunately, many accept the teachings of their parents, pastors, bible school instructors and never compare what they are learning with the pure Word of God. The idea is that if someone is teaching the Word of God, he or she must be teaching the truth. Without a doubt the Word of God is the truth, but some teachers are wrong, and teach what they think is the Word but in reality is just the ideas they have developed on their own apart from the inspiration of the Holy Spirit. Consequently, just as the servant who buried his talent viewed the Lord as being gratuitously cruel, many people today are similarly deceived. Others however think of the Lord as a God that could never be capable of disciplining His servants since they are also His children. Many people think that a good father would never physically discipline his children and so they project that view of human fatherhood onto God. It is necessary to know how God has revealed Himself through His Word in order for us to have a proper idea of how He deals with His people, His children and His servants.

The truth is that the Lord is a loving God that looks at His servants and children through the eyes of love. However in Hebrews 12:5-6, the Word also affirms that the Father disciplines the children that He loves and that it is a fearful thing (from the Greek *phoberos*: also meaning terrible) to fall in the hands of the living God (Hebrews 10:31). God addresses His own people in these passages not unregenerate sinners. While it is true that unbelievers come under God's judgment, they do not "fall into the hands" of God.

The emphasis of the entire parable is on the servant that buried his talent. Why did this servant bury his talent?

One distinct possibility is that he considered it insignificant. In his thinking, that talent would neither help nor hinder the work as a whole. Remember he was a servant just like the others. He did not just sit around twiddling his thumbs until his master returned, he was busy doing something, just not what he should have been doing.

Many Christians today have never even considered that someday they will have to give an account of the spiritual care of the "talents" (souls) for which they have been entrusted. Even if they do have a clue to the spiritual responsibility they have in caring for souls, they reason that their contribution will neither help nor hinder the church of which they are a part. They reason, "What I do is so little, so insignificant next to all that is going on in this church."

Those who accumulate more talents are usually the most faithful. Permit me to use financial giving as an example. Make no mistake; finances are not only material things. Finances, riches, money, material wealth are all very spiritual matters that have eternal consequences. It is a mistake to treat this subject as non-spiritual. Some people think that the poorest members of the church are the most faithful in returning their tithes. This is usually a mistake with the exception of the other extreme the richest, who often think their tithe is too big for the church's needs.

Quite often those members who are less financially prosperous with smaller incomes and thus a smaller tithe, reason that since their part is so small (in monetary value), that it will make no difference in the income of the church. They think that the quantity is so irrelevant that it will not be any help. The mistaken vision in this example is that financial giving and the paying of tithes is to "help" the church. For them the matter is the absolute monetary value. God however does not consider the monetary value that each one returns, but the measure of faithfulness of each servant. Hypothetically, the brother that earns $1,000 per week and pays a tithe of $100 is just as faithful as the brother that earns $10,000 per week and pays a tithe of $1,000. That is what happened in the parable: the one who receive five talents produced another five, the one who received two another two. Both were faithful in doubling their initial amount, the proportional amount entrusted to each one.

The truth is that those who have just one talent run the greatest risk of being unfaithful, by being unwilling to pay the price of growing and developing in the work. They imagine that merely attending church services on the weekends, singing some hymns, and paying their tithe is enough. Many even go to the point of affirming that it is the pastor's job to involve himself in the work of the Lord for the furtherance of the kingdom, since he has received more talents and takes a salary from the church to get the work done. This is a serious mistake because the Lord will require an accounting of each servant for the proportional measure of what He entrusted to them and not the quantitative amount that they received.

Many times those who receive more talents are those who seek more and strive to multiply their talents without regard to any title that they may receive in the body of Christ. God will not only judge us by what we have done, but also by what we have not done. The problem of the servant that buried the talent was not what he did, but what he did not do.

God is interested in our faithfulness. In the Parable of the Workers of the Vineyard, we learn the criteria by which God will reward us. The reward will not be according to how much we have done, but according to how faithful we have been to the Lord. There is a difference. Some may do more than others do and gain the same reward, because they showed the same degree of faithfulness.

In the parable of the workers in the vineyard, all the workers received the same salary irrespective of the duration of time they worked. Some people, who read this parable, conclude that there is no difference in rewards and that there will be no distinction among the servants. I believe however that the bible teaches that there will be. One of the goals of this parable is to show that the reward of those workers will not be for how much they worked, but for how faithful they were. In the same way, it shows that the reward does not depend upon the amount of time of conversion. Some convert at twelve years of age, others at thirty and others just before death. Does this suggest that those who come to the Lord first will have a greater reward? No, not necessarily, it all depends on the degree of their faithfulness.

Suppose that I hire a laborer at five in the afternoon and he finishes his agreed upon task at six o'clock after just one hour. We can say that he was faithful. Now suppose that I had hired a person at eight o clock in the morning to do the same task and he stopped at noon and walked off the job without finishing his task. Should he receive the same amount as the first? Of course not! Although he worked for three more hours than the first worker that I mentioned, he was not faithful. Therefore, I will not reward him but will penalize him. The point here is not the need to do something to gain a reward. The main point here is if you were faithful with what I gave you to do or not.

Suppose that God gave me the responsibility of a pastor and that He gave you the responsibility of a small group leader. God will require of each one of us according to the proportion of what we have received.

But he who did not know, yet committed things deserving of stripes, shall be beaten with few. For everyone to whom much is given, from him much will be required; and to whom much has been committed, of him they will ask the more. (Luke 12:48)

And to one he gave five talents, to another two, and to another one, to each according to his own ability; and immediately he went on a journey. (Matthew 25:15)

If you remain faithful as a small group leader with ten members and I remain faithful as a pastor of a church of 100 members, who will receive the greatest reward? Neither one, we will be equally rewarded. It is a matter of faithfulness in that to which God called each one of us.

Another reason why the servant may have buried his talent is that he had a wrong perception of things. The servant whom the Lord called wicked and slothful thought that talents were for people, when, the truth is that they are for the Lord. The heart's desire of every faithful servant of God should be to do everything within his ability to multiply the talents that God entrusted to him to please the one who has called us.

Another possible reason that the last servant buried his talent was because he was ashamed of it. He felt embarrassed to use only that one talent. How many people have received a talent from the Lord, but because of their reputation, they neglected to trade with it? The Lord called the apostle Paul who wanted to minister among the religious Jews to a ministry to the pagan Gentiles. This apparently was not Paul's preference. He felt he was uniquely qualified to reach the Pharisees and doctors of the Law. Paul could have revolted against this but he perceived God's purposes and remained faithful to God's purposes through his ministry. He could have buried his talent but he did not and God greatly used him as a result.

Yet another reason why the servant may have buried his talent was that the act of trading involves risk and hard work. In the Bible to burry something, is symbolic. The servant buried his talent in the earth: this speaks of the force of worldliness, of the power that the things of this life have to smother the talents that God has given us. The love of the world has the power to bury our talent. When we involve our heart in the things of this world, we stop developing and fulfilling the purpose for which we have been called.

The act of trading in this parable implies faithfulness in the use of our stewardship. Each person receives at least one other person to spiritually care for as a steward of God. We can only build up and multiply our stewardship when we practice it. This is what the priesthood of the believer means. Not only pastors and paid church staff must care for souls; every member of every church has this responsibility. God has called us to minister as kings and priests, ministers of God (minister simply means servant). Every born again Christian should raise and develop at least one spiritual son or daughter. God did not compose the members of His church to make up a club or organization but constituted them as a body, each member having its specific role in multiplication for its continued growth. If you have never done so before, stop and think who has God given to you to develop in the church?

We must be careful not to confuse responsibility and function with position. There are brothers who want to do things in the church as a function of a natural structure, with a title for their position like for example, leader of children's ministry, or administrative pastor. The position is not important, the talent is important. The position should never determine or limit the talent.

There are people in the church who have a position and a title but who exercise no spiritual care in raising up God's children. Similarly, there are people in the church who faithfully exercise spiritual leadership but occupy no official position nor possess any title. So just as there may be no talent to accompany any given position, there may be no position (in man's eyes) to accompany any given talent.

Let us now consider how the Lord judged each one of His three servants.

> *But he who had received one went and dug in the ground, and hid his lord's money. After a long time the lord of those servants came and settled accounts with them. (Matthew 25:18-19)*

The Lord Jesus is coming to reckon with His servants. Most churches do not often teach this truth. However, the Word shows that He is coming to reckon with each member of His body.

> *For we must all appear before the judgment seat of Christ, that each one may receive the things done in the body, according to what he has done, whether good or bad. (2Corinthians 5:10)*

We will all appear before the Judgment seat of Christ to receive the good or bad that we have done through the Body. If our works are good, we will receive a reward. If we have done evil, God will discipline us in that Day. In light of these facts, we should live in the fear of the Lord as far as the works that we practice are concerned.

> *So then each of us shall give account of himself to God. (Rom. 14:12)*

In case you are wondering about where the blood of Christ that covers all sin comes in concerning this matter consider this: God has forgotten everything that the blood of Christ has washed. However, whatever God's people have not confessed to before Him, or whatever sin they have not genuinely repented of, remains written down before God. For the blood to work in our lives, it is necessary that there be confession and repentance of sinful acts and disobedience. To confess a sin not only means that we acknowledge our sin but that we agree that it is offensive and unacceptable to God. The danger for many Christians is spiritual oblivion and a seared conscience that otherwise would lead to repentance.

> *If we confess our sins, He is faithful and just to forgive us our sins and to cleanse us from all unrighteousness. (1 John 1:9)*

> *He who covers his sins will not prosper, But whoever confesses and forsakes them will have mercy. (Proverbs 28:13)*

How about you my friend, how is your life before God? Many Christians, instead of recognizing the error of their sin, and repenting before the Lord, justify their attitudes by coming up with all sorts of varied excuses for why it just is not practical for them to obey the whole Word of God literally in all situations. As a pastor who has counseled hundreds of church members, I have concluded that most everybody imagines that their special circumstances excuse them from fulfilling the obligations that the rest of the body of Christ should fulfill. In other words, they always seem to find an excuse for not repenting and practicing what God has called them to do. God sees and records all of this, since the blood of Christ does not cover any sin whenever there is no confession and repentance.

Scripture indicates that as Christians we must be open and transparent, placing every failing, sin and disobedience under the blood. If this is not done then we will pass through the judgment seat of Christ and Instead of receiving rewards we will be disciplined and although we will still be saved, it will be a salvation as of by fire (1 Corinthians 3:15)

In the Word of God, there is a sequence in the Judgment of God for believers: the first step is the blood. If we confess and believe on the Lord, His precious blood washes us. If we keep falling, this shows slavery in our lives. From the blood then we will need to advance to the cross, which is the next step in the sequence. God nailed our old man to the cross and freed us from slavery to sin. However, God through the Judgment Seat of Christ will treat whatever sin or failure the blood and the cross have not resolved. He will correct and deal with us in relation to sin in our lives.

> So he who had received five talents came and brought five other talents, saying, 'Lord, you delivered to me five talents; look, I have gained five more talents besides them.' His lord said to him, 'Well done, good and faithful servant; you were faithful over a few things, I will make you ruler over many things. Enter into the joy of your lord.' Matthew 25:20, 21

The Lord said the same thing to each of the faithful servants. Now the Lord is watching and looking for the level of faithfulness of each one of His servants.

Some people think that pastors, missionary workers and other leaders have done a lot here on the earth. In addition, many have done more and greater works than even Christ did in His mortal body. I believe that what we do here is just a preparatory training for what we will be doing in the millennial reign of Christ. What we do today is "the few things", but as we are faithful in these "few things", God will qualify us and place us over the "many things", later.

Consider how the Lord rewarded the faithful servants. What a joy it is when God rewards us! What a joy it is when God approves us! Do not allow yourself to think that the approval of God is a small thing. I personally believe that God made us all with a craving for approval, for attention. We did not get that from Satan, although his thirst for glory and recognition was the driving force that motivated him to desire the position of God and got him kicked out of heaven. This "bent" for approval and recognition can lead us far from God but it can also draw us near to Him if we value His recognition above that of all others.

I can see in my two sons how they have responded to my recognition through the years. My firstborn is quite a musician. He took music lessons as a small boy, learned music theory on the piano, and from there took a few guitar lessons and taught himself how to play the most difficult guitar riffs in modern music today. Whenever he learned something new, he would always want to show my wife and me how he mastered part of a solo. Of course, we always gave him a healthy dose of recognition and together with the recognition of his friends and admirers he went on to learn how to play, the base guitar, piano, saxaphone, drums, violin, and the flute.

My youngest son today has distinguished himself as bible teacher. His mother and I gave him approval at a very young age but he assimilated our approval as just being considerate and kind parents. Today because he has advanced and gained recognition from others, he has grown much more.

Approval is powerful! On the other hand, we can argue that reproof is the worst thing that a person could go through short of going to hell. History and research have shown us that reproof and lack of approval is fatal to the human soul. Therefore, the reward for the faithful is approval of God: hearing His voice bragging on us is the sweetest music in the universe.

Christians who find this argument overly sentimental and even carnal in emphasizing of the value of God's approval of His children, should examine themselves and consider that they may have some deficiencies in their own self-identity. Let's face it; a healthy self-identity is a gift of God. A troubled and overly exalted or overly despised self-image is the scourge of servitude to Satan. If receiving human approval is a joy to our children, imagine the effect of receiving praise from the mouth of God will have upon them.

Just think what that day will be like! Imagine entering through the gates of glory and contemplating a countless multitude of saints. Suddenly you hear your name, and the Lord publicly declares "Welcome, good and faithful servant!" That would be a marvelous situation wouldn't it? I don't know about you but I want to hear that from my Lord, I want Him to approve me! I have learned to live with the desire for His recognition as one of His faithful servants. In case you feel inclined to judge me as being driven by "man-centered" motivation as opposed to God centered, let me just remind you that it is God who has made these promises. We should not despise them!

With all due respect to my dear brothers who understand true Christian humility, I find it tiresome to have to listen to certain self-avowed "bible teachers" and arm chair internet theologians who teach that we should just forget about ourselves and strive to be expressionless nobodies so that the Lord can be exalted on High. Listen, the Lord can hold His own among those of His children and servants who know who they are in Christ! I am not diminishing the need to exalt the Lord, but emphasizing the need to recognize that He is exalted through what He is able to do through you and me! It is ridiculous to imagine that someday the Lord will publicly approve someone who is stuck on themselves and hungry for glory. Yet hunger for the approval of God is the most biblical motivation out there.

I hunger for His approval because I love Him, Just as I hungered for my father's approval because I loved him and my sons hunger for my approval because they love me. I have come to recognize that I have received a talent from the Lord, and for that reason, I am inexcusable. My goal is to be available to God and to have a heart to multiply these talents, obeying God's call on my life so that on that day He approves me to reign with Christ through the entire thousand years of His reign.

Now consider the punishment of the wicked and slothful servant.

> *"Then he who had received the one talent came and said, 'Lord, I knew you to be a hard man, reaping where you have not sown, and gathering where you have not scattered seed. And I was afraid, and went and hid your talent in the ground. Look, there you have what is yours.' But his lord answered and said to him, 'You wicked and lazy servant, you knew that I reap where I have not sown, and gather where I have not scattered seed. So you ought to have deposited my money with the bankers, and at my coming I would have received back my own with interest." (Matthew 25:24-27)*

This wicked servant heard what nobody ever wants to hear. God called him wicked and slothful. In the same manner that there will be public approval from God, there will also be public disapproval and even discipline from the Lord. If the public reprehension of man is bad, imagine receiving the public reprehension of God. The interesting part is that the last servant mentioned in the parable, was startled and shocked once his master confronted him, because he did not think that he had done anything wrong. He never thought that his master would reprove his work. He did not speak with the Lord as if he had done something wrong. In his thinking, he did what he felt was acceptable, he put away and keep the talent safe that he had been given. As he returned the talent, he felt that he was proving his faithfulness in returning, that which was the Lords. He most likely even imagined that He was flattering the Lord by calling him sever and austere. Yes, he was completely surprised when he heard the displeasure of the Lord who called him wicked and slothful. However, he must have quickly recognized his error as the Lord exposed the folly of his fake argument and excuse for his negligence. This servant was a believer just like the other two, but he was not a faithful believer and God judged him based on the quality and lack of his works.

In Luke 19, Luke repeated this same parable with additional details. In Luke's account, there were three types of people: the faithful believer (good and faithful servant), the unfaithful servant who hid the talent in a cloth and the enemies of the king, whom He had executed. The proof that the unfaithful servant is a believer is that he was not included among the enemies of the king.

> *Therefore take the talent from him, and give it to him who has ten talents. For to everyone who has, more will be given, and he will have abundance; but from him who does not have, even what he has will be taken away (Matthew 25:28-29)*

Here we have a play on words. The servant who has fruit will have more; and the one who has no fruit, even the little that he thinks he has, will be taken from him. The Lord is looking for fruit in our lives.

> *'And cast the unprofitable servant into the outer darkness. There will be weeping and gnashing of teeth.' (Matthew 25:30)*

This verse speaks of three things: darkness, weeping and gnashing of teeth. First, I want to suggest the need to observe that this darkness does not refer to hell. There is no verse in the entire bible that refers to hell as darkness. The bible says that hell is a lake of fire and brimstone, a place of eternal damnation, but never calls it darkness.

Secondly, we need to understand the context of what is happening. In this moment, the Lord sits on His throne judging His servants. The Glory of the Lord is upon His throne. When the Lord said to cast the unprofitable servant into the outer darkness, he goes to a place of darkness because he is leaving the place of the glory of God. This darkness does not refer to damnation, but to exclusion from the presence of the Lord, of His glory, for a time. There are servants that God will exclude from His presence.

Then there will be weeping and gnashing of teeth. This weeping is not the weeping of Hell. Since there will be so much suffering in Hell I do not imagine that anyone will have the luxury of weeping there. Imagine weeping in a bon fire! You could scream, but weep? While on fire? I don't think so. No, this weeping is of repentance. This gnashing of teeth points to the lamentation of an unfaithful servant who has come to understand the folly of his unfaithfulness as he chastises himself saying, "I had a chance to do what I should have done, but I didn't, I had the opportunity to serve and I didn't serve."

This portion of the parable troubles some people in the Church, because it is so much more comfortable to think that the Lord is referring to the unsaved. However, I suggest that we challenge this thinking as biblically erroneous. We have seen that the servant was a believer because his master had purchased him and judged him together with the other servants who were faithful with their talents.

There is nowhere in the Bible where believers are judged together with unbelievers. This judgment refers to the judgment seat of Christ, when He will judge all believers. The faithful servants will receive a reward and the unfaithful will receive severe reproof. The servant who buried his talent was not a false servant, but a true one. However, his lord disciplined him for his unfaithfulness and his negligence. There is a difference between a false servant and an unfaithful servant.

The will of God is that we enter into the joy of the Lord, but many have buried their talent. Many do not even know they have a talent much less know what it is. They can only think of the church as a structure, an organization. They do not think of the Church as the bible reveals it: as a body with members each having a vital function necessary for growth and edification. There are no members without a function!

What a need there is today to change our attitude concerning the work of God, so that there is fear and trembling, and not the slumber of negligence. Above all this, we need to understand that we must deal with any sin of omission or commission in our lives today.

I sincerely hope that you do not finish reading this chapter feeling fearful, depressed or uneasy. My goal is that by reading these words, you come to have a new readiness to become a faithful servant of God. If you are prepared to trade your talent, the Lord will be gracious to multiply it in your hands, so that you may see the work of your hands, and the fruit of your labor. My prayer is that God finds both you and me faithful before Him, the angels and the saints that will be present on that glorious Day of the Judgment seat of Christ, as good and faithful servants, qualified to reign with the Lord for a thousand years when He will rule over this earth. Let us be exhorted by these considerations to multiply our talents!

CHAPTER 5

A BIBLICAL VIEW OF REWARDS

As was stated in the previous chapter the Lord has shown through scripture that the subject of rewards is very important. For this reason no rewards offered or promised by God should be despised. The subject of rewards in the New Testament is positively taught in 43 instances in 16 New Testament books. Jesus spoke on the subject no less than 16 times and other New Testament writers (Paul, Peter, John, and the writer of Hebrews) spoke 27 times on the subject. Once again I feel compelled to mention that mankind has always been geared towards rewards.

If we are completely honest, all of us can identify with the desire to be rewarded. At the same time we need to be careful to not confuse the sanctification of this desire with the repression of it. God has placed certain desires within each one of us and we need to recognize that the first sin of mankind was committed through the perversion of this desire. Religion seeks to repress legitimate desires while redemption in Christ seeks to lead us into the sanctification of each and every one of our human desires. Let us observe how each New Testament writer spoke on the subject of rewards.

In Matthew 5:12 Jesus summed up the conclusion that those who suffer for the name of Christ should be glad.

> *"Rejoice and be exceedingly glad, for great is your reward in heaven, for so they persecuted the prophets who were before you."*

Jesus exhorts those who suffer for the sake of the Gospel to rejoice and be glad in their suffering and He sites two motives. This is important! Jesus knew what was in man. He is God and He knew the makeup of those that He created. Jesus could have very easily exhorted those who suffer for the sake of His name without making any reference to any reward. He could have just said: "Yes, you will suffer, yes it will be difficult, but I am worth it. Prove your love for me by submitting to the suffering that comes your way because of me." He could have spoken in such a manner and there would be no fault in doing so. But my point is that He didn't do that. He said rejoice and be exceeding glad.

Luke adds "Rejoice in that day, and leap for joy: for, behold, your reward is great in heaven". He mentioned two things to explain the motive for the rejoicing. The first: great is your reward in heaven. If Jesus Christ the Son of God listed reward as motivation for suffering because of His name, who are we to condemn such motivation? Jesus said great is your reward in heaven. When Jesus says something is great we should recognize that there is what I consider great and what you consider great and then there is what Christ considers great. Great according to Christ, must be unimaginably great as far as our imagination can go. Eye hath not seen nor ear hath heard the things that the Lord has prepared for us. When Christ says to rejoice and be exceeding glad because great is our reward in Heaven, I say "Praise God for His unspeakable reward".

In the very next phrase Jesus gave another reason to rejoice and be exceeding glad: "for so persecuted they the prophets which were before you". Christ is exhorting all those who suffer for the sake of the Gospel because they will be recognized together with the prophets. In effect Christ is saying that there will be great reward and great recognition. Once again, Christ didn't even mention that a motive for suffering for His sake was the privilege of suffering in His name, instead He mentioned a great reward and a great recognition in Heaven. Even Christ Himself didn't suffer only for the sake of suffering, nor even only to obey God, for we read in Hebrews 12:2 "who for the joy that was set before Him endured the cross, despising the shame, and is set down at the right hand of the throne of God."

Christ went through the ordeal of the cross because of the joy that was set before Him: the reward for His sacrifice. What was His reward? You and me, and all those who have accepted His redemptive work, not to mention that in Philippians chapter two Paul mentioned that after "he humbled Himself, and became obedient unto death, even the death of the cross. God also highly exalted Him, and gave Him a name which is above every name." Even Christ received reward for doing the will of the Father. Rewards are of God!

Later in the Sermon on the Mount Jesus continued speaking about rewards: In Matthew 5:46 He said:

> *For if you love those who love you, what reward have you? Do not even the tax collectors do the same?*

Previously in verse 43 He reminded the disciples that He was addressing that which they had been taught that they should love their neighbor, and hate their enemy. Then He told them in verse 44

> *"But I say to you, love your enemies, bless those who curse you, do good to those who hate you, and pray for those who spitefully use you and persecute you,"*

And why should they do this? He continued in verse 45:

> *"that you may be sons of your Father in heaven; for He makes His sun rise on the evil and on the good, and sends rain on the just and on the unjust."*

These are at first glance curious words. That ye may be the children of your Father? Can you imagine someone telling you to do something so that you may be the child of your father? If you have a father, you are already his child. Or does a child have to do something to be considered a child of his father? Taken with the next phrase about the Heavenly Father making the sun to rise and sending rain on the just and the unjust we can learn that Jesus is telling His disciples that the reward for loving our enemies is that we will take on the likeness of our Heavenly Father and will be recognized as such by God the Father.

In John 1:12 the apostle stated that as many as received Him, to them He gave power to become the sons of God, even to them that believe on His name. It is interesting to note that all those who have received Christ have been given power (ability) to become sons of God, but it doesn't say that they automatically become the sons of God, but in the Sermon on the Mount Jesus tells us how we can become the children of our Father in heaven: by loving our enemies. This is a promise of recognition as being sons of God, in His likeness. Not all sons are recognized as being in the likeness of their father.

In Matthew chapter six Christ taught about reward for giving alms. He said:

> *"Take heed that you do not do your charitable deeds before men, to be seen by them. Otherwise you have no reward from your Father in heaven. Therefore, when you do a charitable deed, do not sound a trumpet before you as the hypocrites do in the synagogues and in the streets, that they may have glory from men. Assuredly, I say to you, they have their reward. But when you do a charitable deed, do not let your left hand know what your right hand is doing, that your charitable deed may be in secret; and your Father who sees in secret will Himself reward you openly."*

Why do some people give alms and make it a point that others notice what they are doing? The answer is so that they receive the glory of men. The motive is recognition. Jesus didn't exactly even condemn this motive. He merely pointed out that it is a relatively small reward. Then He explained how to give alms so that the Father would reward them openly before men. The implication is that the reward is much greater when we give alms as God prescribes. It is notable that the motive that Jesus sought to promote wasn't even for the sake of the poor but for the giver to receive an open reward at a later time for giving alms so as not to be seen at the time they were offered. It almost seems that Christ wasn't concerned about noble motives but selfish ones, albeit patient and longsuffering selfish motives.

I believe this was done not to discourage noble motives, noble motives are part and parcel of our new nature, but the reality is that God recognizes that they aren't strong enough to be our only motivation. If God had to wait for our noblest motives to move us to get His work done, His purposes would be slowed down even more than they are now.

God is gracious enough to meet us at the level of motivation that will move us to accomplish His will at a quicker and more energetic pace, for the love of those who we may reach while we work for our rewards. Let's face it, if we are honest with ourselves even in light of rewards, we move too slowly. We must recognize there is much land that we must yet conquer for the Kingdom of God and the "days are evil". Therefore we should make the most of each opportunity that the Lord places before us.

Prayer and fasting are also activities that have the promise of reward. Once again it is Jesus Christ who offers a reward for those who pray and fast according to His direction.

"And when you pray, you shall not be like the hypocrites. For they love to pray standing in the synagogues and on the corners of the streets, that they may be seen by men. Assuredly, I say to you, they have their reward. But you, when you pray, go into your room, and when you have shut your door, pray to your Father who is in the secret place; and your Father who sees in secret will reward you openly. Moreover, when you fast, do not be like the hypocrites, with a sad countenance. For they disfigure their faces that they may appear to men to be fasting. Assuredly, I say to you, they have their reward. But you, when you fast, anoint your head and wash your face, so that you do not appear to men to be fasting, but to your Father who is in the secret place; and your Father who sees in secret will reward you openly."

Once again Christ contrasts the small reward of the religious hypocrite and the recognition that such a person receives with the greater and public reward for those who pray and fast as Christ taught. That isn't even including the answer to prayer that we are promised to receive when we pray according to God's will.

So precious is this principle of rewards that Christ even mentioned rewards for "small favors" done to His servants. In Matthew chapter 10:41,42

"He who receives a prophet in the name of a prophet shall receive a prophet's reward. And he who receives a righteous man in the name of a righteous man shall receive a righteous man's reward. And whoever gives one of these little ones only a cup of cold water in the name of a disciple, assuredly, I say to you, he shall by no means lose his reward."

Even a cup of cold water is sufficient to bring a reward! This speaks volumes of how we should see life. Each day we have the opportunity to express the love and grace of God and "be a blessing" to someone. Just the privilege of blessing others is a reward, so much the more knowing that God pays attention to each act of kindness we show in His name.

Unequal Rewards for Unequal Service

Now once we get over the difficulty of admitting that receiving rewards is a spiritual matter and not reserved for the least noble among us and that God even encourages the idea of working for heavenly rewards, it is necessary to also recognize that God doesn't treat or reward individuals with a collective point of view. God will treat every child, every begotten spiritual son, on the basis of his ability and faithfulness with the opportunities that he has been given. This implies that God will distribute unequal rewards for unequal service.

It is interesting to observe the attitude that the world assumes in each generation. In these first decades of the 21st century there is an ever growing attitude that it is somehow wrong or immoral to encourage competition, so that some win and other's lose. The level of education has fallen so much in the United States that many young Americans are barely literate yet make it through school. The "system" can't bring itself to make the poor dears face up to failure if they don't study properly during their formative years in school.

In recent years, we have witnessed the deplorable attitudes of unionized schoolteachers who get the best employee benefits without having to show any competence in exercising their profession. This just shows the despicable attitude that modern society has nurtured in these people so that they think that somehow the rest of the working class of society owes them because they have the right to have privileges that others do not receive.

We are in a societal movement that preaches rights rather than worth. Honest working people have been shaken down so that those who refuse to work for a living can have food and transportation. You can always tell what is antagonistic to the character of God by observing what is valued by secular society.

Want more examples: A beauty pageant contestant is disqualified to take the crown because she thinks that gay marriage is inferior to heterosexual marriage. The rules have just been changed. It isn't enough that women used to be judged principally by their physical beauty as if they had anything to do with that, now they have to embrace tolerance to any and all types of lifestyles condemned by biblical standards and praise that which is reasonably repulsive to the mainstream members of society. The world of the 21st century rewards cowardice, and lack of conviction. The only tolerated convictions are those that mirror the values of the "high priests" of worldly society (homosexuals, hair brained Hollywood movie stars, and eastern mystics among other anti-Judeo Christian types of individuals.)

It all comes down to a hostility to the thinking that we will receive in proportion to what we are able to do and produce and to what we have been given to start with: or in other words: there will be unequal rewards for unequal service.

Jesus laid it out in simple language:

> *"For the Son of Man will come in the glory of His Father with His angels, and then He will reward each according to his works." Matthew 16:27*

Let's consider the context of this statement by looking at the three previous verses:

> *"Then Jesus said to His disciples, "If anyone desires to come after Me, let him deny himself, and take up his cross, and follow Me. For whoever desires to save his life will lose it, but whoever loses his life for My sake will find it. For what profit is it to a man if he gains the whole world, and loses his own soul? Or what will a man give in exchange for his soul?"*

It is absolutely fundamental to recognize to whom Jesus was speaking here. He said this to His disciples: "If any of you decides to be my follower (naturally no unregenerate man would think of following Christ) you must deny yourself first, then take up your cross and then follow me." This is the cost of following Christ. To qualify as a follower of Christ one has to deny himself. Christ has no use for those who wish to preserve themselves. Through Christ's words we can perceive that He would really prefer that we don't even begin following Him unless we are clear that we will have to give up our own preferences and prejudices.

The cross is an instrument of death, a symbol of the constant need of the disciple to die to his individual self. This is the price that must be paid to follow Christ. However along with the price that must be paid to be a disciple there is also a reward attached to it. Not only that, if one doesn't pay the price of denying himself and "losing himself" for the sake of Christ, he will only end up losing it while all the time trying to keep it. In other words, every man will lose his life one way or another. The disciple is given a choice, lose it now, and get it back latter with reward, or try to keep it now and lose it later with punishment and discipline and a sense of loss. Even if we were able to gain the whole world, Jesus added, it wouldn't be worth it, we would still lose everything forevermore. Or in other words, the most you can have now is the whole world, but for how long? Is it worth a thousand years of loss in the kingdom? You be the judge.

When the Lord returns, according to our text in Matthew 16:27, He will reward every man according to his works. Are you ready for the return of the Lord? Are you prepared for the lot you have earned in the kingdom? I suspect if you are like me, you will want to invest more of your life, material goods and energy in multiplying the talents you have received from the Lord.

CHAPTER 6

THE RACE, THE FIGHT, AND THE CROWN

In 1 Corinthians 9:24-27 we read:

> *"Do you not know that those who run in a race all run, but one receives the prize? Run in such a way that you may obtain it. And everyone who competes for the prize is temperate in all things. Now they do it to obtain a perishable crown, but we for an imperishable crown. Therefore I run thus: not with uncertainty. Thus I fight: not as one who beats the air. But I discipline my body and bring it into subjection, lest, when I have preached to others, I myself should become disqualified."*

There are several passages similar to this one in the New Testament that teach us some important things about the life of God's children. The life of a Christian is like a race, a fight and a striving for a crown.

THE RACE

It is perfectly correct to claim that the Christian life is like a race. In fact it is a race. It is a race against time. It is a race with an objective. It is a race that demands preparation and it is a race that brings reward to those who finish it victoriously. The error is in imagining that salvation is like a race. Salvation is neither a race nor is it like a race.

How silly it is to imagine that the all-knowing and wise God could be capable of choosing metaphors that defy common understanding. Who in their right mind would think of participating and winning a race as a valid metaphor to describe salvation? The only possible application would be in the case of some cruel sadistic predator who would take a group of people and line them up side by side and explain that upon hearing the starting gun shot all of them should run as fast as possible because all of them would be gunned down except the person who crossed the finish line first. To equate salvation with winning a race is to accuse God of threatening us with eternal damnation unless we finish in first place. Salvation would be a win or burn proposition. Honestly, what other kind of accusation could a person be leveling against a god who would do that? No, salvation is neither a race nor like a race. Nevertheless we as God's people are in a race so it is expedient that we understand exactly what the race is and why we should run to win it.

The apostle's exhortation is to first of all recognize that no one, not one person in the church can legitimately exclude himself from this race. He asked the question: ". . . Know ye not . . . that all run?" This means that every child of God, every born again member of the church is expected to be running. You my friend are in this race! Are you running? If you don't understand how this applies to you right at this minute, you are in danger of making a grave mistake! All run! All are in the race! There is no question about whether you need to be running or not, for all run!

Can you imagine a race of twenty athletes after the starting gun has already fired and only two or three runners started running? Five or six gaze in the direction of those who left the starting blocks, some stare up at the clock already counting down the seconds of the first few minutes of the race. Some are tying their shoes, some are sitting on the track, some are still doing their stretching exercises and a few even decided to take a nap. Yet others are giving each other high fives but they are not running! Ridiculous! What do you imagine the organizers of the race would be thinking? What about the fans who come to cheer-on their favorite runner?

This scene would be a total and complete scandal! But this is a glimpse of the state of the church! Many have heard of this race, but they are ignorant of the fact that they are on the race track at this very moment! You, are on the race track. Are you running? Why not? All run! Besides the fact that all run, all are exhorted to run the fastest. Not just as fast as they can, but faster than all the others can. The imagery that the apostle is trying purposely to invoke upon his readers is not that of a friendly jog where no one is keeping score. No! The example is of a number of runners all of whom have trained and prepared to win the race, to beat all the other participants, not only to run as fast as they can, but to run faster than all the others. All run! And all run to win! This is what the Christian life is: a race run to win.

Then the apostle Paul explains what this means for each athlete. Every runner strives for the mastery and is temperate in all things. An athlete either needs to learn tremendous self-discipline or he needs to find a competent and demanding trainer and submit himself to the rigors determined by his trainer.

This means that the Christian life is a life of discipline, of hard work and training and exercise. Athletes learn to limit even their social lives and hobbies. Their purpose as an athlete must spill over to each and every area of their lives. Their sleeping habits are affected. Their eating habits are affected, their leisure time is affected, their relationships are affected. Their entire existence is molded by their purpose as an athlete. And just what is that purpose? To receive a crown, or more specifically in Paul's example, a garland of flowers placed on the winner's head and a victory ceremony. In other words their purpose for all the effort and discipline is glory and recognition. In the case of Paul's example in the text last mentioned the crown was a glory and recognition that quickly faded with the drying up of the garland that symbolized the glory of the victory. But in the case of Christians, the apostle taught that the purpose was to receive an incorruptible crown.

I know that this may sound strange to many, but the apostle Paul taught that the motive for running the race is to receive a crown. In the worldly system of secular society the crown quickly fades. Paul argued however that the crown that awaits the Christian who runs and runs to win, paying the price to take first place is a superior crown, a crown that will never fade away, a crown that will endure the passing of time.

A crown is a symbol of recognition and glory and that is exactly what Paul was teaching: that athletes go through all their discipline and sacrifice to receive a corruptible crown. The motive is recognition and glory. Some achieve it through athletics, others through academic degrees. Some achieve honor, recognition and glory through music or song. Others are idolized (glorified) through the recognition of Hollywood through film and television. Some people excel in business and investments and receive recognition and praise for their productivity and business acumen. However, all of this recognition is but a corruptible crown. Athletes grow old and their records are broken by newer generations of athletes. Academic leaders also fade away and are forgotten as younger prodigies take their place. Movie stars and pop sensations lose their charisma and beauty and are replaced by newer sensations. Successful business entrepreneurs also lose their position of prominence as younger professionals rise up to prominence and eventually dwarf them. Someone better will always come along. In this life, crowns just don't last very long.

The desire for recognition is something that God has placed within us. We should not imagine that the desire to win and excel is something that didn't have its origin in God. It is a mistake to think that this is something that Satan has placed within us. Satan can't create anything, he can only corrupt and twist, pervert or suppress that which has been placed in man by God. More often than not the desire to excel is a drive that Satan seeks to suppress in man. He convinces millions of Christians that they will never amount to much of anything and shouldn't even try. It is also true that he perverts this desire and makes monsters out of some people but the fact is that the desire to win and receive recognition is a God given trait. God placed a desire for glory even in His angels. Otherwise the fall of Lucifer would not have been possible. Satan's problem was that he didn't submit his desire to be glorified to God. God was very generous with Lucifer and gave him tremendous honor and glory. His error is that he wanted God's glory as well. The problem of fallen mankind is not his desire to be crowned, or to be recognized since that is what God made us for in the first place (Romans 8:30).

The problem is the pursuit of glory and recognition through illicit and carnal means, which only lead to corruption. The fundamental truth behind this whole argument about rewards is that God's rewards are superior, and the path to those rewards is not the path that fallen man ever chooses. Only those children of God with a renewed mind understand and take the path to God's infinitely superior rewards. But make no mistake, rewards are from God, and every Christian would do well to recognize the surpassing value of striving for God's best and His accompanying rewards.

THE FIGHT

Not only is the Christian life a race but it is also a fight. The apostle

Paul likened himself to a boxer, a prizefighter. This not only speaks of training and discipline but also of strategy and force. A race demands a toned body, quickness and endurance, but a fight requires quick reflexes, perception, strength and aggressiveness. Running a race requires aggressiveness with one's own body but fighting requires aggressiveness with one's own body before the fight and aggressiveness with the opponent during the fight. Paul speaking figuratively of the prizefight explained that he did not waste his energy throwing punches in the air. His attitude was to throw a punch or a series of punches to knock out and eliminate the opponent.

One of the most important attitudes of a prizefighter is aggressiveness. Caution is important but caution alone, while needful to avoid a defeating blow from the opponent, never did win a single fight. Paul was expressing his example of self-discipline and aggressiveness against resisting forces that could get in the way of his victory and his prize. We know this because in the last part of verse 27 he stated that he willingly went through all this sacrifice so that after having preached the gospel he would not disqualify himself. It is so important to have a firm conviction that he was not speaking about losing his salvation. Just think, if the apostle Paul had doubts about whether he would make it to heaven or not, where would the rest of us be? Once again, the apostle's fear was of the possibility of disqualifying himself from the race and the fight. Heaven is not a prize it is a gift. Salvation is not a prize it is a gift. No one can disqualify himself from receiving a gift or else it would no longer be a gift.

Here we see that it is not enough to preach. Paul preached the gospel, healed the sick, suffered persecution and many other things that most Christians would almost never think necessary and yet he saw the need to force himself and buffet his body so that he could finish the race as a winner. The correct attitude that we must learn from Paul's words is that we must be faithful in doing the best we can while always aiming to do even above that which we have done and can do. For this, faith is an indispensable necessity.

The Christian life beyond being a race and a fight is also an all-out war. Besides being athletes and spiritual heavyweight boxing champions, God also calls the Christian to be a good soldier. In Matthew 11:12 Jesus taught that since the days of John the Baptist until now the Kingdom of heaven suffers violence and the violent take it by force.

Implicit in this statement is the application of resistance. The truth is that the Church of Jesus Christ is an invading force in the world. In Psalm 115:16, the psalmist declared that the heavens are the LORD'S: but the earth He has given to the children of men. At the fall, man yielded the ruling rights over the earth to Satan who became the god of this world. We know this because when Satan tempted the Lord in the desert at the beginning of His ministry he offered to deliver all the kingdoms of the world to Jesus if He would bow before him. Jesus never questioned whether Satan had this right or not.

In 1John 5:19 the apostle John wrote:

> *"We know that we are of God, and the whole world lies under the sway of the wicked one."*

That is because Satan is governing through his minions of demons over the world system, governments, the press, education, etc. According to 1 Corinthians 15:45 and 47 Jesus became the last Adam and the second man: a new spiritual head, and under His "headship" the Church, which is Christ's body, has been authorized and sent to take back the earth for God's purposes. When the Lord said to Peter "upon this rock" referring to Peter's confession of the Lordship of Jesus, He would build His church and the gates of hell would not prevail against it, He was revealing that His purpose for the church was conquest, a re-taking of the earth from the clutches of the evil one. The meaning here is not that the gates of hell are moving in on the world and the Church is trying to fight them off. The correct idea and imagery is that the church is the invading force and the church is taking the battle to Satan's strongholds, the gates of his city. The church is the invading force and the gates of Hell will not be able to withstand its strength and violence. Nothing short of this aggressive attitude on the part of the Church will do! Satan will not peaceably give up what he has previously usurped.

The Apostle Paul explained to the Ephesian church that the nature of our battle is not against men, kings, or nations but against an organized army of demonic spirits who occupy strategic strongholds in the world. The truth is that Christ has defeated the enemy and has broken his hold on the world. The job of the Church as the army of God is to take the world back, soul by soul, family by family, city by city, and nation by nation. Our struggle is against real and dangerous enemies but the Lord has already won the war and secured the victory and has opened the path for our own victory. Even so, we must fight courageously and violently against these enemies in order to take back that which rightfully and originally belongs to man.

The fight, the battle and the war are all related. The individual fight is part of the battle of each member of the church. Again, the object of the conflict on any level against Satan and his forces, whether it be personal, family, local church, city, regional or national is to advance the rule of the Lord and is not a question of preserving or protecting eternal life or salvation.

When Jesus explained that those who enter into the kingdom of Heaven take it by force, He was making an indirect reference to this conflict. This conflict began in the days of John the Baptist. Before John, the Kingdom of God consisted of the Jewish state. There had been no prophetic voice from God to His people for more than 400 years until John began preaching that the Kingdom of heaven was at hand. There has always been a conflict between Satan and God's people. However, with the preaching of John, something new began to be established.

The kingdom of heaven is the specific part of God's kingdom, which will fully manifest itself during the millennial reign of Christ. There is the appearance of the kingdom, which Jesus taught about in some of His parables, and this consists of everything that appears to be of His rule. The appearance of the kingdom is important because the kingdom definitely has its characteristics that must be visible. However, there is the problem of mere appearances without real heart attitude.

This "heart attitude" accompanied by a righteous pattern of works can be called the reality of the kingdom. The appearance of the kingdom would be the visible church and all those who claim Christ as their Lord while the reality of the kingdom is everything that goes beyond mere appearance and cuts to the heart. Jesus spoke of the reality of the kingdom to His disciples in the Sermon on the Mount.

Finally, there will be the manifestation of the kingdom. Christ explained in the text of Matthew 11:12 that those who have the reality of the kingdom are the ones who violently fight against the enemy in the spiritual realm. The fight is fundamentally on the spiritual level however, it always manifests itself through its effects on our body and soul. The Christian solder has a mind transformed by kingdom values. The emotions of the Christian soldier are under the discipline of the spirit and the will has disciplined itself to choose the will of the Father in each circumstance. Then of course, the body has been made a slave so that when it is necessary to go without sleep, food, affection and comfort, so that the work of God prospers and advances, the body will not succeed in mounting a revolt against the will of the spirit.

Christians usually consider violence as a negative trait and that God's people should be gentle and never violent in their dealing with others. However, some types of violence are needful in the Christian life. While God gives salvation by grace through faith to His children, the advance of the kingdom of heaven only occurs through battle. Our battle is not against flesh and blood but against principalities and evil spirits operating on different levels of power and authority. It is only in resisting, in applying force against these evil spirits that God's kingdom advances. Never think that if the church, which is the body of Christ and the army of God does nothing, that Christ's rule will advance, it will not. The expansion of the Gospel is not automatic. God is sovereign but He never works apart from His people. That is the reason we are still on the earth; we have not yet finished our work.

Expanding the rule of Christ, edifying the body of Christ, obeying the great commission are all one in the same and none of this happens without violence in the spiritual realm. When we as the people of God begin to recognize that, we are already in a battle and that God calls all of us to fight as soldiers, we will be able to understand and avoid many difficulties in the Christian life.

There are Christians who are apathetic, paralyzed and passive in many situations where God calls upon them to be strong and courageous. Unfortunately, many have been convinced that living in the age of grace means that they need not do anything through the body. Some go as far as saying that God does not desire or expect sacrifice. Once again, we need to be very clear: grace is for salvation but violence in the spirit is necessary to advance the work of God. In reality, this violence is only a working out and maturing of the grace that we have received starting with our salvation. Those who do not learn this lesson will never fully see the blessing of God upon their lives, because they imagine that conquests and victories come in the same way that salvation comes – by grace.

While the complete manifestation of the kingdom will take place after Christ's return when He sets up His millennial kingdom, the reality of the kingdom of heaven is already present as Christ explained in the days of John the Baptist. However, the church establishes the kingdom on the earth by taking possession of spoils held by the enemy as a group of soldiers does in an invasion. These spoils speak of anything that the enemy has seized at some point that God had originally given to His people.

In Matthew chapter 12:25-29 we read:

> *"But Jesus knew their thoughts, and said to them: "Every kingdom divided against itself is brought to desolation, and every city or house divided against itself will not stand. If Satan casts out Satan, he is divided against himself. How then will his kingdom stand? And if I cast out demons by Beelzebub, by whom do your sons cast them out? Therefore they shall be your judges. But if I cast out demons by the Spirit of God, surely the kingdom of God has come upon you. Or how can one enter a strong man's house and plunder his goods, unless he first binds the strong man? And then he will plunder his house."*

In the last part of this section of Christ's exchange with His Pharisee critics who questioned the source of His power to cast out demons He spoke of a strong man, his house and his goods. The strong man is Satan and his minions. His house is wherever he has been able to take over. It could be a person, a family, a group of people, a place or region. Satan is a thief, so the strong man's goods represent things he has stolen from God's people.

These stolen goods can be people, spouses, sons, daughters, relationships, health, prosperity, self-esteem, identity, and even success in ministry. Jesus was explaining that in order to cast out a demon or a demonic influence, someone would have to bind the strong man. This "binding" speaks of engagement in spiritual battle.

This spiritual engagement in battle against evil spirits involves a proper understanding of who God is, who we are as God's people and His agents on the earth, who Satan and His demons are, and what they are and aren't able to do and what we are and aren't able to do against them. To sum up: God is all-powerful, all knowing and sovereign. We are His agents on the earth. The enemy comes only to kill, steal and destroy. Christ came to give life and life abundantly. The Father has given Him all authority and He has called us to go and make disciples and spread His rule through the earth.

We as God people have been commanded to preach the gospel, baptize those who believe, make disciples and teach them to heal the sick, cast out demons and anything else necessary to destroy the works of the devil. The gates of hell will not be able to withstand Christ's heavenly kingdom that is invading the earth through the Church, which is the body of Christ and the army of God. This understanding is foundational but beyond that, there is the need to maintain the proper attitude.

The Lord told Joshua as he was preparing to enter into the Promised Land to "be strong and of a good courage" three times in the space of twelve verses. Fear not! Be strong! Believe! Go ye! Stand firm! Resist the devil! God has given commands such as these to His people all throughout the centuries. Without this attitude and the proper knowledge of the nature of the battle that God has placed us in, we will not be able to advance the kingdom of God on the earth. The only thing that slows God down is His people and their ignorance and lack of a proper attitude. This attitude, which is so often lacking, is nothing more than a reasonable reaction of faith to God's attributes and purposes.

Whenever we encounter the strongman, God expects us to bind him, enter his house and take the spoils that he has stolen. The Lord taught us to pray that God's will be done on earth as it is in Heaven. Whenever we encounter a situation that God does not permit in heaven, we must resist it violently in the spirit, and overcome the demonic resistance until God's forces reverse the situation and it conforms to His will as it is in heaven.

Jesus continued later in the same chapter speaking of the nature of demonic activity. In chapter 12:43-45 we read:

> *"When an unclean spirit goes out of a man, he goes through dry places, seeking rest, and finds none. Then he says, 'I will return to my house from which I came.' And when he comes, he finds it empty, swept, and put in order. Then he goes and takes with him seven other spirits more wicked than himself, and they enter and dwell there; and the last state of that man is worse than the first. So shall it also be with this wicked generation."*

Either we understand that we must take the kingdom of heaven by force and in this war we must use violent tactics where the best defense is an advancing attack through which we take the conflict to the enemy, or we will open ourselves to the humiliation of an enemy occupation. We must either advance against Satan and his forces or he will find us, move into our house and drag us into a worse situation than he had us in previously. Jesus called those who have been able to break free from Satan's clutches but fail to advance and overcome him, a "wicked generation". This was because their passivity and cowardice permitted the enemy to return and take back that which God had originally forced him to give up.

Here is what this battle looks like: While the imagery that Jesus seemed to invoke through the example of an unclean spirit re-taking an empty and swept house points to a re-possession or a demonic possession, in practice, evil spirits take full possession of individuals only in rare cases. I do not believe that it is necessary that any child of God should have to "share" a house with evil spirits but the fact is that the Apostle Paul commanded his readers in Ephesians 4:27 to "give no place to the devil". The reason being is that he will always take any territory that we neglect or fail to protect.

Take yourself for example, in II Corinthians 10:4 were Paul teaches us

> *"For the weapons of our warfare are not carnal but mighty in God for pulling down strongholds, casting down arguments and every high thing that exalts itself against the knowledge of God, bringing every thought into captivity to the obedience of Christ."*

Strongholds are thoughts and ideas that the enemy brings into our mind. Once we permit one demonically conceived thought to enter in our mind and allow it to remain, the enemy will continue to bring in other thoughts that build upon each other as bricks laid one on top of another in the construction of a wall.

Now the first thoughts seem innocent enough, because the enemy knows that if we identify the source of the thought as originating in him, we will resist it and expel it from our mind. The Word of God teaches that we must discern these things. The greatest spiritual battlefield is the mind. If the enemy can get into our mind and enter our thought process, then he can control large portions of our lives. How does he do this? The answer is that he brings in one thought at a time like a brick layer setting bricks one alongside of the other, row by row building one wall then another until eventually an entire brick building has been erected. That is what a stronghold is; it is a castle built upon hundreds and thousands of thoughts, ideas, and lies. It is easy to toss out a brick, but once we permit the enemy to build an entire castle of bricks, it is not so easy to toss the whole thing out.

A few years ago in Brazil a Christian father complained to me that he could not get his teenage son motivated to do anything with his life. He complained that all the boy did was surf the internet all day long. He had no interest in learning how to drive and did not like to play soccer like most Brazilian young men. He lost interest in going to church services and he just stayed home in front of the computer all day long.

Now I know both this father and his son. They are both born again Christians. However, there are some major spiritual problems in their home. The biggest problem is in the mind of the father. His relationship with his son is not the only problem area in his life. He also has serious marital problems. While he is an above average business man, he knows how to run his business and turn a good profit while keeping honest and obeying all the laws of commerce and taxation, his family life is a disaster. His home is not a combat zone in the sense that his wife and son have arrived at the point of throwing objects at each other, but spiritually the house is full of "trespassers". I am talking about evil spirits. That is correct, evil spirits in a Christian home! Folks, it happens, and it is much more common than you think.

In counseling this brother, who I have chosen just as an example because his is a classic case, just one among so many others, when he complained of his son's inactivity and internet addiction, my first reaction was quick: just change the password, and there will be no more internet access. He just laughed and said that would cause even more problems. "Yes", I replied, "but it would solve the one you are complaining about." In his mind, he was a hostage in his own home. He felt powerless to confront his own son and lay down the law. The enemy somehow through a series of thoughts planted in his thinking was able to build a stronghold of lies that prevented this brother from assuming his God ordained role as head of the family. When I tried to tell him that he had the authority to lay down the rules in his home, he could not properly "hear" me because there was a huge castle in his head. It was as if I were outside with a sledgehammer. I could knock holes in the castles walls all day long but he would have to hear me out and allow me to correct him for some time before this fortress would start to crumble and the rubble could be cleared away.

This process requires humility and patience. It does work, but the longer a person has allowed the enemy access to his thoughts, the longer the process of freedom and victory will take. The example given is just one among a myriad of possibilities. On the personal level of conflict, the enemy may have gained access in any number of other areas. The enemy holds many Christians captive in the areas of finance and employment, others in a maze of health problems, some in diverse types of addiction: tobacco, alcohol, drugs, sex, entertainment, gambling and the like. Some have problems in general because of improper self-image. Nothing seems to go right for these people. They love the Lord, desire to do right but they have become victims of demonic strongholds in their thinking.

This demonstrates why discipleship is so important in the church. It is through the discipleship dynamic in relationships that we can most effectively identify and confront strongholds. This is because true discipleship strives for growth not just friendship and acceptance. Without discipleship structures among Christians I am pretty much convinced that the enemy will eventually be able to disable and dismantle any local church as a threat to his kingdom. The good news is that freedom and victory are available. While there does have to be effort on our part to enter into this "inheritance" God's grace is available for this also. I will share more about the role of discipleship in securing our victory as Christian runners, fighters and soldiers in chapter 9: "Building a spiritual inheritance".

Aside from being a race, a fight and a war, the Christian life involves a striving for a crown.

THE CROWN

I have already mentioned that the objective of the race and the fight is a crown, a reward, and now we will examine what the Word of God teaches specifically about crowns.

In I Corinthians chapter 4, the Apostle Paul wrote to the Corinthian believers about the proper way to view God's ministers. The truth is that God calls all Christians to be ministers in God's service. However, often Christians harbor the notion that God constituted the Church with members who just come together and sit in the pews while a select group of a more dedicated class of Christians serves them by handing them the weekly bulletin, passing the offering plate, singing in the choir, and preaching a sermon to them. Nowhere in the scriptures can we find such a model and as long as a great number of Christians imagine that they have no responsibility in and to the local church, we will continue to delay the work of the gospel and each church will see only limited fruit. Now Paul mentioned that there were people in the church that were unfavorably judging his ministry and his ministry team. How often do such situations appear in churches today? Not much has really changed since the first century! Paul did not seem to be overly concerned about what others were saying about his ministry. However, he did find it necessary to teach that unless where sin was involved; all ministers in the church are directly responsible to God. God will evaluate the validity and quality of each minister and the resulting fruit and not the members of the church or other ministers. He then warned against judging the work of others.

In 1Corinthians 4:5, he taught:

> *"Therefore judge nothing before the time, until the Lord comes, who will both bring to light the hidden things of darkness and reveal the counsels of the hearts. Then each one's praise will come from God."*

Every Christian can receive praise from God. God chose to symbolize this praise with a crown. Not every Christian will receive praise from God, but every Christian may receive praise depending on whether or not they were faithful and pleasing to God through their ministry as Christian workers. We can cross-reference this passage with the words of Jesus when he taught that not everyone who calls Him Lord would enter into the kingdom.

In Matthew 7:21-23 we read

> *"Not everyone who says to Me, 'Lord, Lord,' shall enter the kingdom of heaven, but he who does the will of My Father in heaven. Many will say to Me in that day, 'Lord, Lord, have we not prophesied in Your name, cast out demons in Your name, and done many wonders in Your name?' And then I will declare to them, 'I never knew you; depart from Me, you who practice lawlessness!"*

WHY SHOULD I BE GOOD? SALVATION IS FREE!

These "many" correspond to ministers and their ministries that call Jesus "Lord", prophesied, cast out devils and performed many wonderful works in His name. In other words, we may declare many ministers and ministries as successful and blessed of God and yet the Lord Himself, may not so recognize them on "that day". The Lord will call these ministers "workers of iniquity". Iniquity is not necessarily immorality or evil conduct. Iniquity is simply "good things" that religious people do, which God has not commanded. Ministers have the responsibility to do what the Spirit of God leads them to do, not what they decide or prefer to do.

Each Christian, each minister of God can look forward someday to receiving a crown of glory for the work they have done in obedience to the leading of God's spirit and His Word. This is a precious privilege. The fact is that if each Christian neglects to fulfill his or her purpose as a minister of God's will and blessing, he or she will reap unpleasant consequences. Therefore, we should not lightly esteem the praise that He bestows on each one who is faithful until the end.

In Philippians 4:1, Paul brought up the subject of crowns when he spoke of the fact that his ministry had fruit measured in souls. He said:

> *"Therefore, my beloved and longed-for brethren, my joy and crown, so stand fast in the Lord, beloved."*

Here Paul called those people who came to the Lord through his preaching as his joy and crown. The highest standard of measurement for Christian ministry today is the number of disciples that each of us has begotten in God and raised up as mature ministers in their own right. Paul reaffirmed this principle again in 1Thessalonians 2:19 where he wrote:

> *"For what is our hope, or joy, or crown of rejoicing? Is it not even you in the presence of our Lord Jesus Christ at His coming?"*

The weight of our crown, which aside from praise from God, is also described as hope, joy and rejoicing, will be measured in terms of the number of disciples that we make during our time here on earth. The great commission is a mission fulfilled by God's people with God guiding the way and lending His power through every step of the way. God does not need us to make disciples but He will make no disciples without our participation. God is so gracious! He provides the guidance, gives the power and when we follow His direction and present ourselves as His tools, He shares His glory with us when the fruit comes. More often than not, we as God's people overlook the glory, the praise, the crown that He so graciously offers us. Why is this so often the case? It is just another example of the difficulty that the very people of God have in understanding and accepting God's grace. Many Christians cannot bring themselves to the point of believing that God saves with no regard to merit. Yet when they do perform some good work in the name of the Lord they imagine that they are somehow paying off a debt for their failures and shortcomings as Christians. They cannot bear to think that it is proper to accept any praise, reward or crown because, in their own thinking, they will never arrive at the point of deserving anything.

In 1Corinthians 15:10 Paul shared his revelation of how the grace of God continues to work in us after salvation.

> *"But by the grace of God I am what I am, and His grace toward me was not in vain; but I labored more abundantly than they all, yet not I, but the grace of God which was with me."*

In salvation, the grace of God works through us when all we do is believe and receive Christ's work for us on the cross. In sanctification and holiness however, Paul understood that the grace of God works through our efforts, our praying, fasting, and our labor. We must work, but at the same time, we need to recognize that it is not just man working! God initiates His work in us, giving us all the resources; His guidance, His wisdom, His power, His Spirit; He provides all the resources to accomplish the task that He has elaborated to the end that He has determined.

The man of God is simply a tool in God's hands. The mind and the hand of the master do the work, but never without the tool. Yet the glorious difference between the illustration of a craftsman and his tool is that a craftsman gets all the glory for his work, but the Christian in the hands of the master craftsman also is included in the recognition and the glory. This is grace, it is unexplainable! It is nothing logical it is just grace!

Not all Christians will receive a crown. This is because not all Christians present themselves as a living sacrifice, holy acceptable to God, which is their reasonable service. In other words, not all Christians present themselves as tools in God's hands. We are children of God called to be

His ministers (His tools). Many Christians either do not understand this or do not accept it. A characteristic of those Christians who understand and accept their role as God's ministers and vessels is that they look forward to Christ's return. In II Timothy 4:7, 8 Paul told his disciple Timothy that he had accomplished everything that God expected of him and was ready for Christ's coming.

> *"I have fought the good fight, I have finished the race, I have kept the faith. Finally, there is laid up for me the crown of righteousness, which the Lord, the righteous Judge, will give to me on that Day, and not to me only but also to all who have loved His appearing."*

Those who have served the Lord faithfully and purposefully in the way and manner that the Lord prescribed in His Word love His appearing! The crown is for all those that love His appearing, His return. Many have no love for the idea of Christ's return. Christians who are busy with their own agendas and projects and would rather that Christ not come so soon. This is not the heart of a true servant of God. God disqualifies such Christians from receiving a crown because they do not care about His work and interests. They have their own priorities. These Christians receive the grace of God to do the work of God in vain because while the power and resources to do the Lord's work are available to them they neglect this grace and remain inactive in accomplishing the Lord's purposes.

Another characteristic of those ministers of God who will receive their crown from the Lord are those who endure testing and hardships because of the Lord's work.

The apostle James wrote in his epistle in chapter 1 verse12

> *"Blessed is the man who endures temptation; for when he has been approved, he will receive the crown of life which the Lord has promised to those who love Him."*

Here the apostle James confirms the words of Paul in stating that God will try, test, and judge all Christians. Only those who endure temptation and the difficulties associated with making disciples are apt to receive the crown of life. This testing necessitates endurance and tears as the psalmist described in Psalm 126:6

"He who continually goes forth weeping, Bearing seed for sowing, Shall doubtless come again with rejoicing, Bringing his sheaves with him."

There is rejoicing, but first there is weeping. These servants of God couple their enduring of temptation with their loving the Lord. Only those who truly love the Lord will patiently endure the testing. Most Christians do not endure the testing even to be trained and molded and shaped until they have attained a pattern worthy of being replicated in the lives of others and thus show that their love for the Lord is limited. However, those that endure will receive a lasting reward at the appearing of the chief Shepherd as Peter attested to in 1Peter 5:4.

"and when the Chief Shepherd appears, you will receive the crown of glory that does not fade away."

Some Christians will endure until the point of death. The words of the resurrected Jesus that appeared to John on the island of Patmos reveal that at least a group of disciples will endure suffering in prison, tribulation and even death because of the gospel. This may very well be the description of the experience of those Christians that were initially not ready for the Lord's coming as a thief before the great tribulation and as a result had to go through the hardships of the persecution of the Anti-Christ. Yet these Christians depending on their testimony during this most difficult time can also enter into the praise and joy of the Lord's crowning glory at the judgment seat after the great tribulation and just before the millennium. John described this experience in Revelation 2:10

"Do not fear any of those things which you are about to suffer. Indeed, the devil is about to throw some of you into prison, that you may be tested, and you will have tribulation ten days. Be faithful until death, and I will give you the crown of life."

Finally, a somewhat sobering thought, is that there is a good chance that there is a limited amount of crowns available to the ministers that have served the Lord down the ages. This makes sense since the kingdom will be limited in scope: on the earth for one thousand years. I would imagine that there will be many positions of honor and glory available for those who will reign with Christ during the millennium but there will not be an infinite amount of crowns. From the words of the risen Lord in Revelation 3:11 we can easily conclude that although at one point we were qualified to receive a crown, it is possible for someone to take it from us. However, this will only happen if someone else becomes more fruitful or more faithful that us, and the Lord decides that he or she would do better in His service than we would.

> *"Behold, I am coming quickly! Hold fast what you have, that no one may take your crown."*

We must remember that during the kingdom age the Lord will be governing through a political system as well as a spiritual one. The Lord's government must be efficient. In order for justice to prevail, His ministers must be the most competent and effective possible. This will necessitate the need to place only the best ministers in each position and responsibility. Today in the church age, the age of grace, many times and in many places the Lord is limited to use inferior ministers.

Men like Noah, who faithfully built the ark during 500 years before the first rain came and destroyed the earth in the flood, others like Abraham, Moses, Joshua, David, Daniel the Apostles, the great reformers and evangelists and thousands of others throughout the ages will be among those that are chose for these positions. The Word teaches us that many are called but few are chosen. These few are the ones that will receive the crowns. While we must admit that relatively few Christians will be qualified to receive a crown, it is of utmost importance that we understand that we all have the opportunity and thus we must heed Paul's exhortation to run the race to win the crown. The sad fact is that very few people desire to run with such force and endurance. However, the invitation has been extended to all.

We have seen that the context of each passage of scripture that we have examined concerning receiving a crown is that of being qualified, of striving, of doing something in order to receive the crown. In no portion of scripture are rewards and crowns, glory and honor associated with salvation. The bible does not support the teaching that all Christians will receive a crown irrespective of their works. This idea is a product of sloppy theology based on an incomplete understanding of the earthly kingdom of Christ and its purpose in the grand scheme of history. So why should you be good or holy if salvation is by grace only? We can add to our answer. Holiness is the only path to a crown of glory in the kingdom of heaven.

CHAPTER 7

THE FEAR OF THE LORD AND HOLINESS

Besides the grace of God and the love of God, another one of His attributes that has been commonly misunderstood is His justice. The concept of justice has been so watered down in modern society that its implications have become almost unimaginable. Absolute justice offers no threat to those who are absolutely just, the problem is, who is absolutely just? Those who lack the recognition of their unrighteousness before the righteous judgment of God are just plain blind.

Before considering the fear of the Lord it is necessary to consider the Lord that should be feared. If we try to discuss the fear of the Lord with those who have little concept of the justice of the Lord we will end up with a simplistic explanation that it just means the "respect of the Lord". But practically speaking the fear of the Lord is more than just respect. Respect is the bare minimum of consideration that we owe toward any person. Think about it, according to the Word of God, mankind was created in God's image. This means that since all people originated from the first man created in God's image every human is a creature bearing God's image. Whenever anyone treats another person with disrespect, the disrespect is aimed at God's image. Therefore respect for fellow humans is merely a basic attitude of decency.

There really is no more virtue in respecting God Himself than there is in respecting His image. Imagine for a minute if you were to have a life size portrait taken of yourself and had a cardboard marquee made up for people to remember you by. If your friends and family get together and draw a bulls eye on your cardboard face and throw darts at it would you feel respected? What about a simple portrait placed in a frame and hung on the wall? Wouldn't you be a victim of disrespect if people that passed by your portrait drew a mustache on your image, or a pair of spectacles or any other type of defacement? Imagine walking through the White House in Washington D.C. and seeing the former president's portraits defaced by the tourists that walk it's halls. Yet disrespect for God's image abounds. No, the fear of God isn't simply respect! It is our lack of ability to reconcile the grace and love of God with His justice that makes it hard for us to imagine that at the same time God is to be feared.

The same God that told Adam and Eve that the day they disobeyed His command to not eat of the fruit of the tree of knowledge of good and evil because they would surely die, the same God that did not give them even one chance to remain in the garden after the fall, is the same God that we serve today. The same God that when king Saul received directions to wait for Samuel and decided to go ahead and offer a sacrifice and as a result was rejected as King with no second chance to correct his error, the same God that caused the ground to open up and swallow the families of Dathan and Abiram and all their possessions because they challenged God's choice of Moses as a leader over Israel, the same God who slew Ananias and Sapphira for lying about the price of the sale of a piece of Land, is still the same God that we serve today.

These and many other accounts reveal an aspect of God's character that deserves more than just "respect". According to the wisest man in history it is the fear of the Lord that is the beginning of knowledge. In other words it is wise to recognize that God is no one to be mocked or slighted much less disobeyed or ignored! There is an inflexibly with God who lays down His righteous laws and never tolerates one instance of disobedience without meting out the punishment promised for the offense. God is to be feared!

There are a number of places in the Bible that mention the need to fear God and His punishment of evil and of unfaithfulness of Christians. While most Christians accept the idea that God disciplines His people, the form that this discipline takes is almost completely vague and undefined. I suggest that the Scriptures reveal and describe this chastising and that this punishment will occur principally in the one thousand year reign of Christ.

Before the Lord began teaching His disciples through His discourse called the "Sermon on the Mount" Matthew mentions at the end of chapter four that great multitudes had been following Him because of His fame as one who produced many miracles of healing. Just before He began preaching on the mountain in chapter 5 verse 1, we read that the Lord Jesus seeing the multitude went up onto a mountain and sat down, then His disciples came to Him. Apparently only the disciples followed Him up the mountain so His discourse was preached mainly to them. There is no indication that the multitude also accompanied Him. In verses 21-22 Jesus taught His disciples saying,

> *"You have heard that it was said to those of old, 'You shall not murder, and whoever murders will be in danger of the judgment.' But I say to you that whoever is angry with his brother without a cause shall be in danger of the judgment. And whoever says to his brother, 'Raca!' shall be in danger of the council. But whoever says, 'You fool!' shall be in danger of hell fire."*

Since the Lord was teaching His disciples when He spoke of one brother being angry with another He was speaking of two Christian brothers in conflict. One Christian calls his brother Raca, which means, a good-for-nothing fool. If a Christian speaks to his brother like this, Jesus taught that he is in danger of hell fire. The Lord wasn't referring to an unsaved person, since an unsaved person will go to hell even if he does not call anyone Raca. Whenever the Bible talks about works, it speaks to those who are already in relationship with God. For those who do not belong to God, there is no need to mention works or deeds. Jesus is speaking of a saved person, a brother, but because he is angry with his brother, he is in danger of hell fire.

Jesus continued in verse 23 saying,

> *"Therefore if you bring your gift to the altar, and there remember that your brother has something against you, leave your gift there before the altar, and go your way. First be reconciled to your brother, and then come and offer your gift. Agree with your adversary quickly, while you are on the way with him, lest your adversary deliver you to the judge, the judge hand you over to the officer, and you be thrown into prison."*

Most Christians today recognize that Jesus was speaking of the principle of fellowship in this passage. In order to have fellowship with

God we must maintain fellowship with our brethren. The problem is laxity in applying the principle because of a misunderstanding of verse 25. In verse 25 Jesus warns that we should quickly resolve complaints and conflicts with our brother before he takes the matter to the judge. Many imagine that Jesus spoke of a spiritual principle concerning fellowship and then left a warning that applied exclusively to the Jewish economy of justice. While Jesus did speak in terms of a temporal process of justice before men in this age and more specifically within the judicial system existent in Israel in the first century, He was speaking prophetically of what will happen in the judicial economy of His Millennial Kingdom reign. Things like this will happen in the kingdom age. The kingdom is very strict. The Lord will rule with a rod of iron! Today is the age of grace. God's grace reigns today in this age. But in that day, in that age, justice will reign, and perfection will be required of those who serve the King.

This has very serious implications, and Christians need to understand fully what it means for them. What often happens is that injustices are committed by Christians against one another and many times neither side in the conflict has the humility to recognize his error or his sin. Since there are times when we are unjustly accused by others many times we assume that no one ever has a legitimate cause against us. This matter is further complicated by the lack of understanding of how sins committed against others are resolved in God's kingdom. Many times there is the attitude that the person wronged should just forgive the offense and nothing further needs to be done. If this was the case Jesus would not have said anything further.

The amount of words spoken by Christ that were recorded in the Scriptures is very small compared to the entire content of the whole Bible. It is a grave mistake to imagine that anything Christ taught in some way has no application to our lives. These words of warning speak to us also. For this reason if we become aware of a legitimate complaint that a brother or sister has against us no matter how petty we may consider it, we should follow His directions for reconciliation. Otherwise God will treat us as the guilty party and there will be judicial consequences. This is a serious matter and it isn't a question of being a true or false Christian. Christ spoke these words to Christians because Christians are often guilty of offending and sinning against one another. The problem is not so much that Christians sin against one another, but that they are either not willing to resolve their sins or don't know how, or don't believe that it is necessary to resolve them. Jesus shows that it is absolutely necessary and shows how these matters can be resolved without judicial punishment. The objective is always reconciliation. In the case of a conflict with someone who is not a Christian this implies in coming to an acceptable agreement to avoid judicial action. In the case of a conflict with another Christian reconciliation is the goal. The problem is that too many times Christians are unwilling to reach reconciliation with their brothers in Christ. Sometimes it is a lack of forgiveness when a Christian feels that he is in the right and insists on holding a grudge against another brother. At other times when the Christian senses that he is in the wrong, it is a lack of humility and he does everything to delay or forget the issue. But it is necessary to recognize how God sees these conflicts and how He will judge them.

One principle will never change and that is that no two people in the Church today who are in conflict with each other can serve together in the kingdom. In the coming kingdom, there will only be love and mercy between those who reign with the Prince of Peace; only those who have shown love and mercy to one another now, during this age will be fit to serve in the kingdom of heaven then. This current age is an age of preparation. If Christians can't get along in unity and love today, they will be disqualified to reign with Christ in the kingdom of heaven. If I am in conflict with a Christian brother, and if the conflict is not resolved and reconciliation achieved in this age, then in the future, either both of us will be excluded from the kingdom, or only one of us will be admitted. It will be impossible for both of us to make it in. In any conflict either one side is wrong, or the other side is wrong or both of them are wrong. It is not possible for any two or more Christians to have an unresolved problem with each other in this age to reign together in the millennial age. The Christians that reign with Christ in the kingdom will all be in perfect unity on all levels. In contrast with how He deals with it in this current age, God will tolerate absolutely no carnality in the kingdom age. It is a mistake to imagine that God will deal with His people in the kingdom age just as He deals with them in the Church age. Today the kingdom of God's foundational operation is spiritual but in the millennial kingdom it will be also geopolitical as well as spiritual.

So if we become aware that anyone has a legitimate grievance against us, or if we cause anyone to stumble, we will be in grave trouble with God unless we quickly resolve the issue. The Lord says that while you are with your brother on the way you have to be reconciled to him. That means that while the both of you are still alive, before the Lord Jesus comes back, you must be reconciled to each other. In this age the Lord deals with carnality in the church with a huge amount of patience, but there will be no patience or any type of tolerance for carnality in the Kingdom age. "While you are with him on the way," the Lord said. If you die, or if he dies, or if the Lord Jesus returns before reconciliation is reached, it will be too late and the case will have to be taken up in the Kingdom age. Since it wasn't taken care of "on the way" meaning in this present age, it will have to be taken care of before the judge. The judge is the Lord Jesus. He will deliver you to the officer. The officer is an angel. And the angel will throw you into prison. The prison spoken of here is not only a figurative "mental" or "emotional" prison as some would like to believe, it is a very real and sever place of punishment that any Christian who neglects to be reconciled to his brother while on the way will have to suffer.

The prison referred to here is equivalent to the hell fire spoken of in verse 22. While I don't believe Christ was teaching that born again Christians will be sent to Hell, if they have any unrepentant and un-confessed and thus unforgiven sins, they will suffer the pain of Hell fire (in the Greek "Geenna" which is different from "Lake of Fire"). Just look at the severity of Christ's words to His disciples in verse 26:

> *"Assuredly, I say to you, you will by no means get out of there till you have paid the last penny."*

Where is this place from where the Lord told His disciples that they would by no means get out? The answer is the prison, the fire. Christ taught that no one will get out unless everything (up to the last cent) has been paid off! There is absolutely no leniency here. In the kingdom age, there will be forgiveness, but only after the guilty party pays the last penny. All Christians have a choice: either you pay now no matter how difficult it may seem, or you pay later. The problem is that things have a way of accumulating and in this age there is grace to "skid the rails" whereas in the next age nothing will be facilitated. We all would do well to solemnly heed Christ's words.

Jesus continued in verses 27-30.

> *"You have heard that it was said to those of old, 'You shall not commit adultery.' But I say to you that whoever looks at a woman*

> *to lust for her has already committed adultery with her in his heart. If your right eye causes you to sin, pluck it out and cast it from you; for it is more profitable for you that one of your members perish, than for your whole body to be cast into hell. And if your right hand causes you to sin, cut it off and cast it from you; for it is more profitable for you that one of your members perish, than for your whole body to be cast into hell."*

The seventh commandment prohibited adultery, but the commandment of Jesus prohibits even adulterous thoughts. In the original language Jesus was referring to someone lusting after a married woman, because He was referring specifically to adultery and not just fornication. It is an adulterous thought directed at another man's wife that Jesus was condemning. In the original Greek the word "look" does not imply a casual look but an intentional impure looking. Jesus wasn't talking about sudden thoughts that dart into your mind. Any serious Christian is subject to such thoughts; they are the flaming darts of the evil one. However, it is our responsibility to resist intentional lusting or desiring. Sudden thoughts are mere temptations, but awakened lust is the acceptance of the temptations. It is important to understand the difference.

If the lust is not removed, if the sin is not dealt with, a person can be subject to an experience of being "cast into hell." Again we must not forget that Jesus spoke these words to the disciples. The Lord speaks to His people about what concerns His people and to those who are not His people about things that concern those who are not His. Christians have the grave responsibility of dealing with their sins. If they allow sin to go unchecked in their lives, though they will not lose their salvation, nor have their part in the Lake of Fire, they may be subject to Hell fire or the Gehenna of fire. This is a distinct characteristic of the gospel according to Matthew.

Now in Matthew 18:6 Jesus, again teaching His disciples warned:

> *"But whoever causes one of these little ones who believe in Me to sin, it would be better for him if a millstone were hung around his neck, and he were drowned in the depth of the sea."*

Are we to seriously think that Jesus was just seeking to use some eloquent poetic language devoid of any seriousness? Should we take the words of Christ as vain and toothless? He effectively taught in this verse that to offend or cause someone to stumble is more serious than being drowned and casts into the sea. Imagine for a minute what a horrible death that would be. For what . . . offending someone? Seems like drastic punishment for such a small offence, don't you think? Yet this reflects the attitude of God. He is such a lover of the weak and vulnerable that the punishment for leading these "little ones" astray seems tremendously harsh in comparison. Apparently among human disputes God is inordinately against aggressors. In verse 7 He continued,

> *"Woe to the world because of offenses! For offenses must come, but woe to that man by whom the offense comes!"*

Whoa! I think I'll stay away from offending others, what about you?

In the next verse the Lord moves in even closer with His penetrating judgment showing that it is not only a serious sin to cause others to stumble but even for you yourself to stumble. Verses 8 and 9 say,

> *"If your hand or foot causes you to sin, cut it off and cast it from you. It is better for you to enter into life lame or maimed, rather than having two hands or two feet, to be cast into the everlasting fire. And if your eye causes you to sin, pluck it out and cast it from you. It is better for you to enter into life with one eye, rather than having two eyes, to be cast into hell fire."*

Remember the Lord had been speaking to His disciples all this time beginning with the question they asked in the first verse of chapter 18. Of course, He used metaphor and didn't mean for us to take the suggestion of cutting off members of our body literally.

When someone cuts off their hand or foot, they can still sin. If you cut off a foot you can still walk with crutches or travel by car. If you cut off a hand, you can still sin with the other one. Cutting off hands and feet and plucking out eyes cannot prevent us from sinning.

So the Lord wasn't speaking of literal hands and feet and other body members, but of dealing with the sin within us and of not making provision for the flesh but removing any provision for it. He did mean to arouse fear of adverse consequences. If you can't seem to control the members of your body then you need to begin eliminating them. It is better for you to enter into life maimed and incomplete than to remain whole and be cast into hell.

Only Christians can sacrifice body members to enter into life. The unregenerate cannot enter into life no matter how many limbs they cut off. In any case they will have their part in the Lake of Fire and their only hope of escaping hell is to be born again. But Jesus wasn't speaking of the Lake of Fire which is eternal damnation when He spoke to His disciples here. However in this age, a Christian may have to sacrifice very precious things in order to enter the kingdom of heaven.

This means that those who deal with their sins and lusts in this age having voluntarily sacrificed things as precious as hands or eyes will enter into life. While those who refuse to deal with their lusts and who are unwilling to sacrifice their precious hands or eyes will be cast whole into hell. Hell here is the Greek "Gehenna" (the place of the future punishment call "Gehenna" or "Gehenna of fire"). This was originally the valley of Hinnom, south of Jerusalem, where the filth and dead animals of the city were cast out and burned; a fit symbol of the wicked and their future destruction.

Although this Gehenna is a fire, it is not what is generally considered the definitive hell or the "Lake of fire" which is eternal damnation. If a person has become a Christian but his hands and feet are constantly yielded to sin, he will suffer the punishment of Gehenna in the kingdom of heaven. He will not suffer this punishment forever, but will suffer it for a time in the age of the kingdom.

In Matthew chapter 10 Jesus called His twelve disciples unto Himself and gave them power over unclean spirits, to cast them out, and to heal all manner of sickness and all manner of disease. He also instructed them on how and where to preach. Then in verse 28 after warning them that they would be persecuted He added:

> *"And do not fear those who kill the body but cannot kill the soul. But rather fear Him who is able to destroy both soul and body in hell."*

Since Jesus was speaking to His disciples what He meant here is that Christians should not fear what others do to their bodies. God is the only one that they should fear, for God has the authority to cast them both soul and body in hell. We should fear God alone who is the only one who has the authority to discipline us after death. We should have no fear of those who can only kill our bodies.

The Lord continued in verses 32 and 33

"Therefore whoever confesses Me before men, him I will also confess before My Father who is in heaven. But whoever denies Me before men, him I will also deny before My Father who is in heaven."

Christians can be divided into two groups: those who confess Him and those who deny Him. Some confess His name while others do not, thus effectively denying Him. Some are willing to be persecuted because of the gospel while others avoid persecution and any type of suffering. Some will be ashamed and conceal their faith preferring man's recognition above God's recognition. Others confess the Lord openly and are ready and willing to be martyred if the Lord so requires. Apparently this is very important to the Lord. We should not shrink from the suffering that comes through confessing the Lord before men. If we do not confess Him we commit a highly offensive sin more serious than many others. The Lord in turn will not confess our names before the angels of God.

These words of Christ about not confessing their name before the angels implies being cast into hell or being thrown into prison as He taught in the Sermon on the Mount. This confessing before the angels is a matter of recognition not of relationship. Christ has relationship with all of His "brethren" but He will not recognize all of His brethren at the judgment. Just as a judge may not recognize even his own son if the son is guilty before the law.

Jesus spoke in a similar manner in Revelation 3:5.

"He who overcomes shall be clothed in white garments, and I will not blot out his name from the Book of Life; but I will confess his name before My Father and before His angels."

I believe that this will happen at the time of the judgment seat of Christ. The book of life where the names of all those who have been born again are written will be opened in the presence of the Lord and His angels. Apparently, at this time, an angel will then read off each of the names written down, and the Lord Jesus will confess some of these names. Those whose names He confesses will then enter the kingdom while those whose names He doesn't confess will not enter. The names of the unregenerate, the unsaved do not even appear in the book of life at all. The names of the regenerate but defeated are included but not confessed when they are called and the names of the regenerate overcomers at the time of the kingdom will be recognized and ushered into the kingdom.

If you are saved your name is written in the book and even though it may be blotted out or marked at the judgment seat, it does not mean that you are no longer saved. Revelation 20:15 says,

> *"And anyone not found written in the Book of Life was cast into the lake of fire."*

This shows us that those whose names are not written in the book of life will be eternally lost and will be cast into the lake of fire. This will happen at the end of the millennium and at the beginning of the new heaven and the new earth. Eternal salvation is secure; it can never be lost since its basis is the grace of God and not the justice of God. But, there is a danger, if we tolerate sin, if we do not forgive others, if we commit adultery, if we cause our brother to stumble, if we are afraid to suffer or to be persecuted, if we are ashamed of the Gospel, and ashamed to confess the Lord, we run a dangerous risk, for the Lord will deny us before the Father so that we cannot escape temporary punishment.

Jesus called this temporary punishment "the hurt of the second death."

In His words to the church in Smyrna the persecuted church, Jesus encouraged the brethren to be faithful unto death. In chapter 2:11 He made a curious statement saying that "He who overcomes shall not be hurt by the second death." Why wouldn't He say that they wouldn't be killed by the second death or die by the second death. Hurt implies suffering but not death. The second death is eternal damnation in the Lake of Fire. Later in Revelation 20 when John writes about the beginning of the 1000 year reign of Christ he says in verse 6:

> *"Blessed and holy is he who has part in the first resurrection. Over such the second death has no power, but they shall be priests of God and of Christ, and shall reign with Him a thousand years."*

Once again the words "over such the second death hath no power" are curiously arranged. Why speak of the second death in these terms as having any power over someone? One would think that death is death. But these two expressions when placed side by side communicate the idea that the second death can have authority over and hurt someone as if it were not only a place or event in time but a principle or dynamic power. This means that God makes a distinction between those Christians who overcome, who do not suffer the pain of the second death, nor come under the power of the second death and those who don't qualify as overcomers who are delivered to the angels and "cast into prison" and hell fire, who come under the power of the second death and suffer it's pain. Although they will not perish eternally in the second death they will suffer the pain of it and come under its power for a time.

At the beginning of the new heaven and the new earth or the final or eternal state, Satan, the world, death and Hades along with all those whose names are not recorded in the book of life will all be cast into the lake of fire. But during the millennium, the carnal and careless Christians will suffer the hurt of the second death when the second death has power over them.

This punishment will not be the same as the punishment that the unbelievers will have; it is not for eternity. If a Christian lives carelessly in this age and if he loves the world and the things of the world, the Lord will discipline him and he will suffer some of what the unbelievers will suffer. This is what Jesus meant in Revelation 2 by being hurt by the second death. The word "hurt" in the original Greek means to injure someone and to damage him, to cause him pain. For those Christians who have not dealt with their sins, they will still suffer the hurt and pain of the second death during the millennium so that by the end they will have been prepared to enter into the eternal state of the new heaven and new earth.

Jesus told His disciples in John 15:2

> *"Every branch in Me that does not bear fruit He takes away; and every branch that bears fruit He prunes, that it may bear more fruit."*

All the branches of the Vine correspond to Christians since no unbeliever was ever a branch in the Vine. In verse 6 He continued:

> *"If anyone does not abide in Me, he is cast out as a branch and is withered; and they gather them and throw them into the fire, and they are burned."*

The branches that bear no fruit will be thrown into the fire and burned. All branches have life, but not all have fruit. Though they have life within them, they have not produced fruit outwardly. The Lord said that these would be cast out, they would wither and dry up, and then be cast into the fire. This shows us that fruitless Christians will be burned in fire.

We can conclude by considering these passages, that if a Christian does not deal adequately with his sins, he will be disciplined with fire. The question of the day should be: How can a Christian avoid this fire? The answer is to understand and heed the many warnings in scripture. Every Christian must deal scripturally with his sins.

One of the blessings of our salvation is the blood provision for the purification of sins. This provision guarantees us that none of the sins that we have confessed, repented of, and dealt with, and made recompense for by and under the blood of Christ can be used against us at the judgment seat. All of these sins will be forgotten no matter how terrible they may have been. But no known sin that we have ignored and forgotten and that hasn't been dealt with will be forgotten by God.

If we have a problem with another person that has not yet been resolved, or if there are things that need to be forgiven but have not been forgiven, or if we have wronged others or sinned against the Lord, we have to resolve these things in a very specific way. At the same time, we have to take these things through the cross and place them under the Lord's blood. Only then will these things be dealt with, and will we be delivered from the coming judgment.

It is not only unresolved sins that will be treated by the hurt of the second death. The apostle Paul in 1 Corinthians 3 taught that any work done by Christians that didn't have its origin in the will of God and in response to His directions will be burned in this fire. In chapter 3:12-15 he taught.

"Now if anyone builds on this foundation with gold, silver, precious stones, wood, hay, straw, each one's work will become clear; for the Day will declare it, because it will be revealed by fire; and the fire will test each one's work, of what sort it is. If anyone's work which he has built on it endures, he will receive a reward. If anyone's work is burned, he will suffer loss; but he himself will be saved, yet so as through fire."

So all Christians will be saved but some will be saved only after passing through the fire of "that day" which is a reference to the day of reckoning or the day that our thoughts and deeds will be judged and we will either be rewarded or disciplined.

The writer of the book of Hebrews in chapter 6:4-10 says,

> *"For it is impossible for those who were once enlightened, and have tasted the heavenly gift, and have become partakers of the Holy Spirit, and have tasted the good word of God and the powers of the age to come, if they fall away, to renew them again to repentance, since they crucify again for themselves the Son of God, and put Him to an open shame. For the earth which drinks in the rain that often comes upon it, and bears herbs useful for those by whom it is cultivated, receives blessing from God; but if it bears thorns and briars, it is rejected and near to being cursed, whose end is to be burned. But, beloved, we are confident of better things concerning you, yes, things that accompany salvation, though we speak in this manner. For God is not unjust to forget your work and labor of love which you have shown toward His name, in that you have ministered to the saints, and do minister."*

This is a description of a regenerate person. He has been enlightened, unlike the unbeliever the light of the gospel has shone in his heart. He has tasted of the heavenly gift. To taste is to experience, "Oh taste and see that the Lord is good" says the prophet. The unregenerate don't taste the heavenly gift or the powers of the age to come. With all this experience the writher of Hebrews adds to his description that they have fallen away which is impossible for those who have never attained a height to fall from. Only Christians can fall away since an unbeliever has never been in any other state but "fallen". Also an unbeliever cannot be renewed unto repentance since unbelievers have no conviction that they should ever repent in the first place. Finally no unbelieving unregenerate person could ever crucify to himself the Son of God afresh, since he has never accepted His crucifixion in the first place.

But what the writer of Hebrews is teaching is that it is also impossible for a Christian who has fallen away to renew himself again unto repentance because this would be the equivalent of crucifying the Lord again and put Him to open shame. What then is the Holy Spirit saying through these words? We know that the sacrifice of Christ is effective once and for all, there is no need for multiple sacrifices and this never happens nor ever will. The blood of Christ and His sacrifice is still effective to save the fallen Christian. So Christ's sacrifice guarantees that no Christian will ever fall away and be lost but also Christ will never be put to an open shame. God is not mocked, the apostle reminds us.

What will happen then? The Christian is like a plot of land that has been cultivated. If after receiving frequent rain this land produces the correct fruit expected by the farmer it will receive blessing from God, but if it bears only thorns and briars three things will happen. Again, this refers to the Christian who has fallen, and has not repented, but has become an apostate. First he is rejected. Many are called but few are chosen. Then he is near to cursing, not cursed but the curse is near, it is a punishment very much like a curse. Then finally his end is to be burned. This burning isn't a total destruction of the plot of land, only the thorns and briars are burned up, then the fire ceases. In the same way the apostate Christian will also be burned, and all that which resembles thorns and briars will be burned up.

Notice that the writer to the Hebrews after explaining this tells his readers that they are persuaded of better things concerning them. Why so? we should ask. The reason is that they were active and laboring in the work of the Lord. God would not be unrighteous to forget this work and labor of love. We know that salvation is by grace, through faith, the writer is not speaking of salvation, he is speaking of rewards and punishment. Those Christians who produce fruit will receive a reward and those who don't produce fruit but bring forth thorns and briars will be burned.

There is one more passage to examine in the book of Hebrews concerning this subject.

> "For if we sin willfully after we have received the knowledge of the truth, there no longer remains a sacrifice for sins, but a certain fearful expectation of judgment, and fiery indignation which will devour the adversaries. Anyone who has rejected Moses' law dies without mercy on the testimony of two or three witnesses. Of how much worse punishment, do you suppose, will he be thought worthy who has trampled the Son of God underfoot, counted the blood of the covenant by which he was sanctified a common thing, and insulted the Spirit of grace?" (Hebrews 10:26-29).

This passage is similar in thrust to the passage in Hebrews chapter 6. Again there is no discussion of any loss of salvation here. The writer is

WHY SHOULD I BE GOOD? SALVATION IS FREE!

stressing the seriousness of the consequences of a sinful and careless lifestyle in the lives of His redeemed people. There is only one sacrifice in Christ, and it is sufficient once and for all. There is no possibility of losing one's salvation and then receiving it again at a later point in time. There is however the certain danger of straying from the gospel and the consequences of this are very carefully stated. There is no more sacrifice for sins but there is a "certain fearful looking for" of judgment and fiery indignation. Notice that the judgment and fiery indignation devours God's adversaries.

Now the backslidden and careless Christians are not God's adversaries so they will not receive the judgment and fiery indignation, but they will receive the "certain fearful looking for" of judgment and fiery indignation. Or in other words they will suffer something similar to what the adversaries of God will suffer: not eternal damnation but temporal punishment and discipline. The reason being is that their trampling of the Son of God and His work is much more serious than despising the provision for sin in the old covenant. Just think, God has graciously given us the opportunity to become His own begotten sons in spite of the fact that we are totally unworthy of deserving anything from His hand. He has given us so much. If we can't respect that, then there will be harsh consequences. If this were not so, God would not be worthy of our respect.

From these different New Testament passages we can begin to have a clearer vision of the future of God's people. One thing can been seen quite clearly, even considering these often considered difficult texts that is for Christians, the matter of their salvation in the new heaven and new earth, all throughout eternity, is resolved. But in the millennial kingdom age there are doubts and controversies. Few people dare to affirm anything about what will happen in this period of time. What needs to be cleared up is the lack of understanding of how Christians are dealt with in the kingdom age.

In the kingdom there will be different levels of authority exercised by different Christians. Some will reign with Christ because they have worked faithfully and have endured persecution, reproach, and suffering. Some may not have endured persecution or reproach and may have never really suffered because of the gospel, yet they have not yielded to a life of sin and have lived in relative purity. Although they have little fruit deserving of reward, they have at least given a cup of water to a little one for the sake of the Lord's name (Matthew10:42). They will also receive a reward, but their reward will be relatively small compared to someone who had paid a great price to spread the gospel.

In the age of the kingdom, some Christians will receive great reward; others will receive varying degrees of smaller rewards and others will receive no rewards. Yet there will be others who will receive varying degrees of discipline. Those who will not receive a reward may also be divided into a few groups or levels.

One group may not even enter into the kingdom at all. The Bible does not tell us where they will go. It only says that they will be kept outside the kingdom in the outer darkness (Matt. 8:12; 22:13; 25:30; Luke 13:28). They will be left outside the glory of God.

Second, there will be many who, in addition to not having worked well, have specific sins not yet dealt with. They are saved, but when they die, they will still have sins which they have not repented of and dealt with. They will still have the problem of un-confessed and unresolved sin in their lives. These believers will be temporarily put into the fire. They will come out only after they have paid all their debts. This will last at most until the end of the millennial kingdom. The exact duration will depend on the righteous judgment of the Lord at the bema seat of judgment.

There are many details that are not evidently clear concerning the future and specifically the Millennium, but I believe that the Lord has revealed in His Word much that has yet to be more fully understood by His people in these last times. Although there are details which have not yet been completely explained, God has given us sufficient information in His Word so that we may know what awaits us as the children of God during the Millennial Reign of the Lord Jesus Christ. For the present we can affirm that the matter of our salvation is quite clear. When a man trusts in the Lord Jesus, both salvation and eternal life are settled for him. But after a person is saved and up until the time when he dies, his works, that is, his failures or his victories, will determine his fate in the kingdom. Our God is a just God. On the one hand, our salvation is free, and all those who believe will have eternal life. On the other hand, we cannot sin at will just because we have received eternal life. If we bring forth thorns and thistles, we will be burned. If we don't learn to disassociate ourselves from our sins and if we don't resolve all sin in our lives, God has no choice but to discipline us in the future. He has no choice but to cleanse us with specific punishments, so that we can be together with Him in the new heaven and new earth and so that He can present us as a people in whom the work that He began has been completed. Some will receive a reward; some will go into corruption, some will be put into prison, and still some will be cast into the fire and be burned. We must take these warnings to heart and understand the gravity of the responsibility as His representatives on the earth.

It is only with this knowledge that we can maintain a proper fear of the Lord. Not a paralyzing terror of God but a healthy fear of His penetrating justice tempered with the assurance that if we honestly and sincerely come before His throne of grace by way of the cross we may freely partake of His tremendous provision of forgiveness and grace.

So why should we be holy if salvation is by grace? We can add to our answer; without holiness, we will have "hell fire" to pay. A proper "fear" of the Lord will spur us on to properly deal with our sins in a prompt and timely manner and maintain a burning zeal to be ever more fruitful and prepared to stand before Him on His throne.

CHAPTER 8

THE CENTER OF GOD'S HEART AND THE VISION OF THE OVERCOMER

In Proverbs 25:2 Solomon declared that It is the glory of God to conceal a matter, But the glory of kings is to search out a matter. The Bible labels the Church as a nation of kings and priests two times in the first part of Revelation, once by the apostle John and a second time by the twenty-four elders. The Lord Jesus is the King of kings, because He is our king and we are called to be kings to reign with Him. There are a number of truths in God's Word that seem to periodically "disappear" from the attention of the majority of Christians.

Luther was the first man after centuries of church history to "rediscover" grace. Years later the principle of the priesthood of the believer was rediscovered. None of these truths have ever been absent from the written Word, but for several reasons, the Lord seems to periodically allow certain truths to be overlooked, only to raise up someone to re-discover these precious nuggets of truth at a later point in time. So this is the nature of God's glory to conceal precious truths, and it is the honor of kings (the overcomers) to search out these matters.

One of these matters which seems to have been forgotten and has somehow slipped out of the collective mind of modern Christianity is the knowledge of God's central goal in creating the universe, the earth and man. Or in other words: What is central to God's heart and will? I asked this question on my Facebook page "Why be holy if Salvation is by Grace?" (http://www.facebook.com/why.be.holy) and invited several pastors and Bible teacher types to answer the question. Judging by the amount of members on the page and the amount of members who answered the question, the great majority decided not to even try to answer the question. Here is a breakdown of those who replied: As of the date of this publication 316 people answered the following survey question:

In five words or less complete this sentence: God's central purpose is . .

Forty-five different answers were given. Here are the top five:

- To have a relationship with us – 127 votes

- To glorify Himself - 30 votes

- To redeem man through His Son – 24 votes

- Whatever pleases God – 16 votes

- To be worshiped by us – 14 votes

Most of the members of the aforementioned page identify themselves as Bible believing Christians, a few are self-avowed atheists and the rest are probably just curious onlookers. From these results then it is reasonable to conclude that most people even among those who claim to be Christians, are not clear on what God's central purpose is. These results should be disturbing because if a reasonable sampling of "God's people" are not clear about what His central plan and goal and His fundamental desire in the whole of creation is, then His good, perfect and agreeable will not be experienced by His people, and this will result in the misunderstanding of His character and intentions and the fulfillment of His wonderful plans will be delayed.

In His Word the Lord has left us with clues as to what is central in His thinking and purposes. Starting off at the very beginning of His revelation to man in the book of Genesis we read that in the beginning of time God created heaven (the universe) and the earth. In the very next verse He began to focus on the earth. The entire universe gets mentioned in half a verse and for the next few chapters God talks about a tiny speck in the universe called "earth". Already we can begin to discern where the center of God's attention and thus His heart is moving: toward the earth. In the next verse (Genesis 1:2) we read that the earth was without form and void. This is strange and completely uncharacteristic of God's nature which all throughout the entire scriptures is described as orderly and excellent. Without speculating in an abundance of details but yet recognizing that God intends that we understand that Genesis 1:2 is a necessary part of His revelation to man we must stop and explain the meaning and purpose of the three phrases in this verse. We can safely say that the earth was originally created with form and order because in Isaiah 45:18 we read:

> *"For thus says the Lord, Who created the heavens, Who is God, Who formed the earth and made it, Who has established it, Who did not create it in vain [tohuw], Who formed it to be inhabited: "I am the Lord, and there is no other."*

Now this Hebrew word [tohuw] is the same word used in Genesis 1:2

> *"And the earth was without form [tohuw], and void; and darkness was upon the face of the deep. And the Spirit of God moved upon the face of the waters."*

The word "tohuw" is from an unused root meaning to lie waste; it has been translated as vain, vanity, confusion, without form, wilderness, naught, nothing, empty place, and waste, never in a positive way. It's several meanings are: formlessness, confusion, unreality, emptiness, that which is empty or unreal (of idols) wasteland, wilderness (of solitary places) place of chaos, vanity.

So if God didn't originally create the earth as being without form and void something made it that way. Some Bible teachers propose what is called the "Gap theory" basically stating that there was a prior creation before God created Adam. Satan was cast down to this earth and ruined it so at one point God came and re-created the earth. Undeniably in the Genesis account several things already existed: the planet earth, water and darkness before the beginning of the seven days traditionally called the creation week.

In light of the clear organization of the text it would be more appropriate to refer to the seven days as the restoration and reordering of the creation as described in verse one. In any case we know that Satan had been previously cast to earth and as a result the original creation had been rendered chaotic and void. God came and "fixed" the earth and prepared it so that it would be habitable, and blessedly so for the sake of man.

Once man was created the language in the text emphasizes the fact that he was created in the image of God (Genesis 1:26,27). In verse 26, after

God stated that He would create man in His image, and likeness, He said that he would have dominion over the fish of the sea, and over the fowl of the air, and over the cattle, and over all the earth, and over every creeping thing that creeps upon the earth. This verse is also fundamental in understanding God's central purpose and the center of His will and heart. What all is included here? Fish, birds and every creeping thing consist of one distinct category, cattle, another, and "all the earth" yet another. Man's dominion over cattle is easily understood. This speaks of man's rule over domestic animals. Man's dominion over all the earth speaks of his ability to use the earth to his own advantage.

But what should we make of man's dominion over fish, fowl and creeping things or reptiles? Man has never been able to domesticate fish. Granted, some birds are kept as pets but in general man does not have dominion over birds and even less so, over creeping things like snakes and other reptiles. It would not make sense then for these creatures to be interpreted as just animals. Satan and his demons are sometimes represented by birds and serpents and so this passage only makes sense if we interpret it as stating that part of God's purpose in creating man beyond having the image and likeness of God is to also have dominion over Satan and his demonic spirits.

In verse 28 after blessing him, God spoke His first recorded words to man which came in the form of a command: "Be fruitful and multiply, fill the earth and subdue it." This was God's original revelation to man: a two-fold command; fill the earth and subdue it.

Now let's just stop at that point for a minute. What has transpired so far in the first chapter of God's revelation to man? We learn that God created the universe and the earth but the universe isn't the center of attention, nor is the earth just a small part of the universe, it is the location where God has focused His attention. God created man in His own image and likeness, blessed him, told him to be fruitful, multiply and fill the earth. We know that previously Satan was cast to earth and apparently made a mess out of it since at one point it became without form and void. This is important because the second part of God's first words and command to man was to subdue the earth. Now to subdue something there necessarily needs to be the possibility of resistance. When God detailed how the earth would be subdued He explained that man would have dominion over the fish of the sea, birds of the air and creeping things. As mentioned before these types of animals live in relative independence on the earth. For the most part mankind doesn't have dominion over these classes of animals. For this reason it is correct to conclude that it is an allusion to classes of evil spirits that inhabited the earth prior to the creation of man. From these details we can begin to put together God's purposes for the earth and His purpose for man in having His image and likeness.

At one point after Satan and one third of the angels rebelled and were cast to the earth, the Lord put order to the chaos that came about with the presence of these rebellious spirit beings. But besides restoring the order the Lord determined to do something more about Satan and his rebellious followers on the earth. God is the ultimate winner! He began to put a plan into place in order to hand Satan an even greater defeat than expelling him from heaven and banishing him to earth. He would create man, a creature that had His image and likeness and through this created being called man, would eventually judge Satan and his forces and banish them to an even more humiliating state: the pit and the lake of fire. God's brilliance in this plan is that He wouldn't even do this directly but through a creature that has no inherit spiritual power of his own, a race of creatures completely dependent on God's power in order to defeat Satan and his forces. Therefore God would magnify His glory, through Satan's rebellion, by giving occasion for Him to create Man as His agent of revenge in answer to the rebellion of the devil and his minions. The manner in which this is to be done is by God through man and his exercise of prayer.

How God uses Man to Fulfill His will

The Bible shows us that God has chosen to work in response to man's prayer. First, God reveals His purpose to man so that man can understand the Lord's intention. Then with the understanding of God's intent man grows in conviction of the need for God's will to be done. Third, man responds by praying to God in accordance with what has already been revealed. Finally, God does His work and accomplishes His purpose in response to man's prayer. This is how God operates on the earth through His people.

A CLASSIC EXAMPLE OF THIS CAN BE FOUND IN MATTHEW 9:36-10:1

> *"But when He saw the multitudes, He was moved with compassion for them, because they were weary and scattered, like sheep having no shepherd. Then He said to His disciples, "The harvest truly is plentiful, but the laborers are few. Therefore pray the Lord of the harvest to send out laborers into His harvest."*
>
> *And when He had called His twelve disciples to Him, He gave them power over unclean spirits, to cast them out, and to heal all kinds of sickness and all kinds of disease."*

First, the Lord is moved with compassion to save, second, He commanded His disciples to pray, third, they prayed, and last, God sent workers and He worked through them to save.

Prayer should always spring from the will of God. He fulfills His will, but He doesn't do it directly; He uses man to cooperate with Him on earth. For this reason He reveals His will to man and commands men to pray. Only after man prays will He act to fulfill His will. This is the function and purpose of prayer and how God operates on the earth.

SATAN'S INDIGNATION OF THE CREATION OF MAN

Imagine Satan's indignation upon strolling into the garden and seeing what appeared to be God. Satan's original sin was declaring that he would be like God, for that he was expelled from heaven and banned to earth. Then what happened? After God cleaned up Satan's mess, He planted a garden paradise and made man in His own image. When Satan saw the man he recognized that God had made something that he always wanted to be but wasn't: the image and likeness of God. And then God gave him (the man) authority over the earth. Satan now saw that his place of banishment and humility would become even more humiliating. Because now a creature who although was created in the image and likeness of God, was confined in a physical and very limited body, hardly a match for Satan's superior and supernatural capabilities. And yet now he understood that this new human being would be his ruler. Now what would he do?

In Genesis 2 God speaks of two trees, the tree of life and the tree of the knowledge of good and evil. These two trees reveal two principles of life. The principle of the tree of life is dependence on God, and the principle of the tree of the knowledge of good and evil is independence and separation from God. The latter is the principal that Satan always works under and must lead man into in order to resist God. God's will is done in heaven, while Satan's will is carried out in the air. Man's will is exercised on earth. Satan soon saw that his only hope to get back at God was to somehow convince man to side with him under the principle of independence and separation from God. As long as man continued eating of the tree of life he would remain united to God and exercise dominion over Satan and all the earth. But if he would eat of the tree of the knowledge of good and evil he would join himself to Satan and be subject to him over whom he was created to have dominion.

We know the story, Satan succeeded in deceiving Eve and Adam followed her in her transgression and both passed into spiritual death which is separation from God. God's will and central plan was temporarily delayed. One of the results of eating of the fruit of the tree of knowledge of good and evil is that man lost his position of dominance over the earth. The whole earth suffered as a result and from that point forward Satan regained his position as ruler over the earth. He became the god of this world and began to try to consolidate his foothold against God's further purposes on the earth through the agency of man. At this point however God had not been taken by surprise, for unknowingly to Satan, He already had a plan to continue with His purposes using the future seed of the very man that originally failed His purpose. After man's fall God prophesied to the serpent with a veiled message foretelling that through Eve's seed He would bruise his head. In other words God would use man to bring forth another "man" who would be the "second man" and "last Adam". This of course was a reference to Jesus Christ the Messiah.

This prophesy and punishment for tempting man is the foundation for God's plan of redemption. The plan of redemption covers most of the great doctrines of the Word of God including, salvation, justification and sanctification. Now remember at this point that none of these doctrines can be central in God's will and heart because they don't represent what God has been doing since before the foundation of the world. The entire doctrine of redemption is a "course correction" or adjustment because of man's initial failure to fulfill God's eternal purposes on the earth. In Romans 8:29 the Apostle Paul revealed a dimension of the eternal purpose of God

"For whom He foreknew, He also predestined to be conformed to the image of His Son, that He might be the firstborn among many brethren."

BEGETTING SONS FOR GOD

Part of the eternal purpose of God can be expressed in the begetting of sons like Jesus. The Father's will is that Jesus be the firstborn among many brethren. God told Adam and Eve to be fruitful and multiply and fill the earth. This of course expresses His will, that man have His image and likeness so that he may subdue and rule over the earth and that he be fruitful and multiply. The problem was that man fell. At the fall man lost his spiritual likeness with which he was originally created. He became carnal and independent while as before he was innocent and fully dependent on God. Since man no longer possessed the full likeness and image of God, he could no longer be used by God to fulfill His will by ruling over the earth and exercising dominion over it, and there would be no reason for him to be fruitful and multiply in this condition. God's desire was to fill the earth with men in His image and likeness, and not with men in a carnal state, so God had to do something.

In Genesis 4:17-22 we are given a summary of the sons of Cain and some of their accomplishments and feats. Then in Genesis chapter 5 we are given a summary of the generations of Adam and his descendants. Again it is important to recognize that no detail in the Holy Scriptures is merely incidental, the Holy Spirit is revealing important details that give insight into what God's central desires are. God made a point to separate the descendants of Adam through Cain and the descendants of Adam through Seth who was born after Cain killed Abel.

The two lineages are expressed in distinct manners. Cain's descendants were distinguished by their accomplishments while Seth's lineage was only expressed in terms of who begat whom, how old they were when they begat their first son, how many years they lived between each son and how many years they lived after they begat their last son. This reveals a paradigm shift between those who seek to please the Lord and those who seek to please themselves.

The descendants of Cain were the movers and shakers, they built things and made objects, they were project oriented while Seth's descendants just lived and begot sons. These two paradigms can also be expressed in terms of those who do things for God and those who beget sons unto God or more succinctly: doing and begetting.

Adam's lineage through Seth is traced until Noah and his sons. God initiated a new beginning through Noah and his obedience to preach repentance and build the ark, not as a monument of greatness or recognition but as a mere vehicle for the preservation of his bloodline. Through the flood God eliminated all the accumulated generations of man who no longer called upon His name but rather whose wickedness attained its full measure, and whose every imagination and thought was only evil continually. Only Noah and his family were preserved. Once again God gave the same command to Noah that He had given to Adam and Eve. In Genesis 9:1 it is written:

"So God blessed Noah and his sons, and said to them: "Be fruitful and multiply, and fill the earth."

However the descendants of Noah did not fill the earth, they remained together and began to corrupt themselves straying further away from the Lord's purposes. Man decided to team up and build a monumental city and religious center. God stepped in and confused their language and they felt forced to split up and migrate in different directions. Then in the same way as with Adam through Seth, the genealogical record follows Noah through Shem on down to Abram. With Abram God initiates His third beginning by appearing to him and announcing that He would make him a great nation, and would bless him, and make his name great; and that he would be a blessing.

This time the lineage remained unbroken and through the line of Solomon, Jesus was born of Joseph, His legal father and through the line of Nathan, Jesus was born of Mary, the virgin through which He was conceived by the Holy Spirit. Throughout the generations God was able to bring His own Son to earth to become the "second man" and "last Adam", formerly called the only begotten Son of God but now the first begotten Son of God. After the crucifixion and just before His ascension Christ gave what is popularly called the "Great Commission" first recorded at the very end of Matthew's gospel account in Chapter 28 verses 18-20.

"All authority has been given to Me in heaven and on earth. Go therefore and make disciples of all the nations, baptizing them in

*the name of the Father and of the Son and of the Holy Spirit,
teaching them to observe all things that I have commanded you;
and lo, I am with you always, even to the end of the age." Amen."*

The central goal of the great commission is the making of disciples, the going, the preaching and teaching and the baptizing are the methods applied to make the disciples. The main principle that is behind all of these activities however, is the spiritual begetting of children for God. This is the great mission that God has now given to the Church which is the body of Christ who is the head. It is called a commission because the mission is impossible without the enabling power of the Holy Spirit of God, yet we must fulfill it. God has invested Himself in this project, this purpose, this central desire of His heart since the beginning. It is accomplished by God through man. The power is of God, the direction is of God, the strategy is of God, all the resources are God's and we also, as His resources are His.

Man is God's key resource, the only resource that possesses its own will. It is a co-mission because God brings man into His eternal purposes and desires and uses men who freely yield their own hearts, wills and lives unto His purposes. This is the meaning of being a disciple. It is with disciples (men and women created in God's image with a heart changed and yielded to God) that the Lord will fill the earth and unite all things under the headship of His Son.

All of those sons and daughters of God who have understood this eternal purpose and center of God's heart and have made the decision to live in accordance with, and for the benefit of this plan, and submit their time, resources and even their own bodies, as living sacrifices are the overcomers who will eventually reign with Christ at His coming and be used to show the entire universe what the world can be when Christ is reigning in every aspect of life on the earth.

With the understanding of what has always been the center of God's heart and mind allow me to suggest a brief outline of what we may call "the Vision of the Overcomer" or a type of roadmap to eternity.

A BIBLICAL DESCRIPTION OF THE OVERCOMER

First let's define exactly what an overcomer is. It has already been shown that all Christians are called to be overcomers and are given the position of an overcomer but not all are overcomers in practice. There may be many ways to define an overcomer but a thorough treatment of the characteristics of an overcomer can be seen in the Sermon on the mount recorded in Matthew 5, 6 and 7.

We can read a description of the nature of the overcomer in the first twelve verses of Matthew chapter 5 often called the Beatitudes. Here we have seven dimensions of the nature of the overcomer.

Overcomers are identified by their humble nature, they are saddened by what saddens God's heart. While they could easily put to shame and humiliate others who haven't achieved their level of spirituality they prefer to exercise meekness and let those who oppose them save face.

The overcomer longs for God's righteousness and groans when he sees man's unjust and evil behavior.

The overcomer is full of mercy and is not judgmental and harsh in his dealings with others.

The overcomer has clear intentions and has no duplicity at all.

The over comer is willing to fight for the truth so that there can be a solid basis for true peace.

Finally the nature of the overcomer is one of steadfastness in the face of persecution, since persecution always seems to find the overcomer.

In the next section of the Sermon on the mount which we may correctly call the decree of the constitution of the Kingdom of heaven, we learn of the influence that the overcomer exercises over his surroundings.

Like salt the overcomer is an agent of preservation against corruption. Like salt he gives flavor to life. Like salt the overcomer provokes thirst. Like salt in days of old the overcomer is a valuable thing. They are truly "worth their salt"!

The overcomer also influences like a bright light on a dark night. Like light, all eyes are on the overcomer. The overcomer becomes a beacon, a guiding light, a defining reality that reveals the true nature of what was formerly hidden in darkness.

Next in the remaining portion of Matthew 5 (verses 17-48) we can learn of the overcomer and his heart commitment to God's law; not as a means to salvation but as a heartfelt reaction to God's good will.

In the first eighteen verses of chapter six we read of the acts of righteousness of the overcomer. In verses 19-34 we get an insight of the overcomers attitude toward material riches.

In the first twelve verses of chapter seven we get an idea of how overcomers treat others, their brothers and their enemies. And in the last section of chapter seven verses 13-29 we see the basis of the life and work of the overcomer with a view to the kingdom. It all rests on doing the will of the Father.

In summary the center of God's heart and will is to fill the earth, the place of banishment of Satan and his demonic followers, with men: creatures who in their own right are vastly inferior to Satan, yet when in relationship with God are capable of further banishing the evil one to the lowest places of humiliation while at the same time declaring the glory of God through their lives and examples. These we call the over comers! And in "that day" when Christ returns to set up His geopolitical reign of one-thousand years, all of creation will testify to the tremendous glory of a rule unhindered by Satan's meddling.

Only those men and women who have heeded the prophetic warnings of Christ through the Apostle John in the letters to the seven Churches, those who have remembered from whence they had fallen, and have repented, and have done the first works, those who have held fast to that which they had already attained until He comes, those who have washed their garments, so that they may be clean and purchased ointment so they may see, and those who have overcome, and kept His works unto the end, only to them will He give power over the nations. This is the adorned bride that will be presented to the universe! What a wondrous time to be alive that will be.

Why be holy if salvation is by grace? We can add to our answer: It is in holiness that the people of God will be qualified to reign with Christ and enjoy the privileges of the ultimate ruling class.

CHAPTER 9

BUILDING A SPIRITUAL INHERITANCE

(How to have 128 million spiritual children)

As a young father and up to the time when our two sons left home to go to Seminary, I never considered myself a very good father. I always loved our sons but I constantly felt like I was far behind the curve as a good father, even though I always felt like my parents did a good job raising me. Even so, when our boys were much younger I regularly wondered how my parents were able to raise my sister and me. I had a happy childhood. My parents regularly disciplined me but I never felt frustrated by them. I never felt any lack of love or attention or support from them. When I became a father, I never felt like I measured up to my parents in child rearing. I made plenty of mistakes in disciplining our two sons. I was not always consistent and felt like it was obvious to them that I was a weak father figure.

After they became teenagers I began to notice that friends and relatives would make comments about how well behaved and disciplined our boys were. At first, I was convinced that these comments were just polite ways of expressing love toward our family, but after a while, I began to be convinced that the compliments were truly sincere. Then in August of 2009 when the two of them moved to central Brazil to attend a two-year pastoral leadership course, I began to discover that I did an O.K. job as a father after all.

Every two months I would travel to Brasilia for pastoral meetings and I would get a ride to Goiânia to spend a couple of days with the boys. I met scores of people who just fell in love with them. It was almost embarrassing. Apparently, they would spend a lot of time bragging about how my wife and I were good parents. I cannot begin to remember how many brothers and sisters, adults and teenagers as well as pastors would take my hand and congratulate me for the excellent young men that our sons had become. I doubt that there is a greater pleasure in life than receiving compliments for the way we raise our children. I know that pride is a sin but I also have experienced what the Apostle Paul must have felt when he referred to his converts and disciples as his crown.

Now the reason I share this is that it taught me something about raising children and making disciples. The great commission is about teaching how to obey the commands of Christ, not about teaching what the commands are or how to understand them. The purpose of child rearing is to prepare our children to be parents and eventually to raise their own children. We do not raise children to make them family therapists. Think how ridiculous it would be to send our children to school to learn how to live in general.

Public education is about reading, writing, arithmetic and the sciences. Traditionally the goal of education has been to teach children how to think, not how to live. We do not send children to school to potty train them, or to learn how to brush their teeth faithfully after each meal, or how to use a fork and spoon. Children learn to walk, talk, have good manners (or unlearn bad manners) in the home, all of these things are the parent's responsibility to pass on to their children.

In the same way, discipleship is teaching young Christians how to live before God and before men. Disciples are taught within a context of a spiritual family how to walk by faith, how to pray and how to read and meditate on the Word of God. Disciples learn how to be faithful and responsible members of a local church, how to be a good husband or wife, how to raise children, how to preach the Gospel, how to cast out demons, and how to pray for the sick. We do not learn these things in a classroom. These are not subjects for Sunday school curriculum.

We learn all of the things I mentioned through a model, an example, a spiritual father figure. My father never gave me child-raising classes. Actually, he never gave me any type of classroom instruction. My father, like all fathers who maintain a physical presence in the family was a role model. He lived, worked, played, rested, got up early to study the Word, put our home in order and molded my character simply by being an example. I suppose he was just doing what his parents did with him. In the same way, I did the same things with my sons that my father did with me.

After I left home, I became an early riser just like my father. It has been over 30 years since I left my parent's home but my wife can attest to the fact that I am just like my father. Twenty years under his roof set me up for life, and the same is true of my sons. I imagine that they will reflect even more of my influence when they marry and begin their own families.

Child rearing is a powerful principle. However, it is also a two-edged sword. When a father fails to be a worthy role model for his children, his failure complicates the development of future generations that proceed from his headship. God has designed us in such a way that we intrinsically develop our own identity based on the way our parents or guardians raised us.

When the father figure is missing in the life of a child there are always unfavorable consequences. One of the strategies of Satan is his attack on the family. He knows that if he effectively mounts an attack on the fathers he can install his misery into their lineage for generations to come. The only hope for a child that has grown up in the absence of a father figure is to at some point humbly receive a surrogate father that is able to communicate the same love and patience that a godly father would show to his own children.

Unfortunately, in the case where a father has been absent or deficient as a worthy role model, the children, while conscious of their own emotional need, develop defense mechanisms that make it difficult to develop the very type of relationships needed to build a proper self-image as children of God. God has provided the father figure to prepare the child for a relationship with God the Father, and the mother as a pattern for the relationship with the Holy Spirit. Ideally, the child receives this preparation from the biological parents but there can be substitutes. The important thing is to recognize that children learn how to develop a relationship with God through the example of the parents.

Interwoven throughout the Old Testament we can testify to the value that God places on the family and child rearing. The goal of child rearing is to bring each child to a level of maturity upon which he or she can make responsible decisions on their own, learning to become independent and eventually interdependent in relation to their parents and other siblings. The classic Old Testament passage on child rearing is Deuteronomy 6:5-7 and reads:

> *"You shall love the Lord your God with all your heart, with all your soul, and with all your strength. And these words which I command you today shall be in your heart. You shall teach them diligently to your children, and shall talk of them when you sit in your house, when you walk by the way, when you lie down, and when you rise up. You shall bind them as a sign on your hand, and they shall be as frontlets between your eyes. You shall write them on the doorposts of your house and on your gates."*

Here we have the Biblical model for raising children. How does it happen? First, the parents must have a complete and thorough love for the Lord. This assures that they will naturally pass on to their children the same love. This is foundational and absolute because if the parents are just going through the motions, they will produce children in the same pattern.

Parents always transmit their character to their children unless there is a substantial separation. Besides having a genuine and profound love for the Lord, a heart-knowledge of His teachings is also necessary. Before teaching anything to the children the commands of the Lord had to be "in the heart" of the parents. From the very beginning, the pattern for the multiplication of human generations depended on the mother and father having a correct relationship with God and His Word. If the parents fail here, they will seriously compromise the whole process.

However, this love and heart knowledge of the Word of God still is not sufficient to establish God's pattern for multiplication. The parents must diligently teach that which is in their hearts concerning the Lord. While it is true that children subconsciously receive many things that their parents pass on to them in virtue of being together, the parents need to diligently and purposely teach many other things.

Parents must cultivate a healthy flow of communication between themselves and their children so that they reinforce their example with words. Finally, the examples and words from the heart need to be present throughout all aspects of family life: time together in the home, outside in the way, rising up in the morning and settling down at the end of the day. The principles of the Word should be constantly before the family to the point of writing them on the walls and carrying them in written form throughout the day. When parents and their children follow this pattern, God can much more easily manifest His favor and plan to the nations.

From this principle, we can begin to understand how the Lord works through the local church to fulfill the Great Commission of making and multiplying disciples. This must be done on the local church level since the Universal Church while a true entity is also an impractical model for disciple raising just as the concept of the entire human family is useless for raising your own children.

Some evangelical writers and church leaders teach that the great commission is the local church's responsibility and not the individual member's concern. This is also an impractical position since any given member can try to push off his responsibility to the remaining part of the local church. This thinking is useless. I am not suggesting that each member of the church treat the great commission on an individual level independent of the local church. However, I am suggesting that it is necessary that each church member be taught to be a responsible "disciple maker" so that if each member does his or her part the whole church will be effective to this end.

While in recent years, many churches have assimilated the restoration of the "priesthood of the believers" into their current church ecclesiology, in practice the great majority of 21st century Christians have no biblically based ministerial function within the church. I am not referring to titles but to functions.

In Ephesians 4:11-16 the apostle Paul outlined the relationship between ministers and the edification of the Church.

"And He Himself gave some to be apostles, some prophets, some evangelists, and some pastors and teachers, for the equipping of the saints for the work of ministry, for the edifying of the body of Christ, till we all come to the unity of the faith and of the knowledge of the Son of God, to a perfect man, to the measure of the stature of the fullness of Christ; that we should no longer be children, tossed to and fro and carried about with every wind of doctrine, by the trickery of men, in the cunning craftiness of deceitful plotting, but, speaking the truth in love, may grow up in

all things into Him who is the head — Christ - from whom the whole body, joined and knit together by what every joint supplies, according to the effective working by which every part does its share, causes growth of the body for the edifying of itself in love."

Traditionally and even in small group or cell group based churches this passage has been interpreted as an affirmation that God raises up ministers and special ministries to fulfill the basic ministerial functions of each church.

The functions recognized are church planting (apostles), prophecy or ministry of the Word (prophets), evangelism (evangelists), pastoral ministry (pastors), and bible teachers.

The common conclusion is that these ministers build up and cause the church to spread as the entire church learns from them as experts. However, this interpretation ignores the remaining portion of the passage where we learn that God gives these "ministers" for the perfecting of the saints to do the work of the ministry. Because of the perfecting process in the saints for the work of the ministry, they edify the body and it grows into the measure of the stature of the fullness of Christ. Therefore what we have here, are the main subjects that each saint needs for his training so that he may do his part in the edification of the body. Each of these "gifts" (ministers) to the church then teaches the curriculum peculiar to his distinguishing ministry. Theologians often call these gifts the five-fold ministry gifts.

So then, the Apostle teaches the entire church how to plant a church. The prophet teaches the whole church how to discern the direction of each work within the general guidelines of the written Word.

The evangelist models evangelistic techniques that each member must learn.

In addition, the pastors and teachers train the body (each member) how to develop a pastoral and teaching ministry. In other words, God calls all Christians to practice all of the ministerial functions whenever the need arises.

Part of the pastoral ministry is to train new pastoral ministers. Even if most of these ministers never receive a title of "pastor" or elder or deacon, the reality is that they are already operating in these ministries. Eventually the church will recognize them as such and will incorporate them as either staff workers or "lay" leaders.

I have learned that beyond recognizing the need for each member to be a minister we must advance and insist that each member be willing to develop into a recognized leader within the church. In order to obey the great commission it is inevitable that each member become the leader of at least one person, the person they are training as a disciple. Discipleship is not only transferring what we are to another person but also transferring our ministerial competence and abilities.

A team of scientists once randomly formed a group of five people, placed them in a boat, and took them to the middle of a lake. Each person in the boat received an oar and the scientists gave the group the single instruction to row the boat back to shore. They gave them no other details as to what side of the lake they should go or who should direct the group.

At first, each person started rowing and the boat just spun in circles since each person was rowing in different directions. Soon they all recognized that they needed to agree on what direction they should row. Different members of the group began suggesting a different direction and finally one of the five took the lead and directed the others to follow his suggestion.

Once the group reached the shore the scientists removed the person who took the lead and took the remaining four out to the center of the lake again and gave them the same instructions as before. This time a different person quickly took charge and directed the other three to the nearest shore. The researchers repeated the process until only one person remained. Of course, if they had taken the last person of the five to the middle again he would have found his way back with no problem.

What this "experiment" reveals is that each time they removed the leader; another leader took his place to complete the task and lead the group. The traditional idea is that the first person to assume the leadership is the leader and the rest are the followers. However, this experiment shows that all are leaders, and under the right conditions, each one will take on the responsibility to get the job done. There are several levels of leadership and some people are reluctant leaders, but all people are leaders. Just think of any area where you have more knowledge or experience within any given group. Within that context, most likely you will take on the function of the leader. In any give circumstance, you may not have a leadership title, but the group will recognize you as the authority in that circumstance or situation. For example if you are a medical student among a group of friends, you most likely will be the designated leader in the event of a medical emergency. All eyes will look to you as the one who has the most authoritative answer until a more authoritative medical figure arrives on the scene. I am sure you would agree that the truth of this example is self-evident.

So what this means for the church is that the idea that not all are called to be leaders must be rejected. Otherwise, the great majority will attempt to assume the position of a follower. It is true that we are all followers but we are also all leaders. Just as everyone is either a son or a daughter, most of them will naturally also become fathers and mothers.

In the Church, we must insist on the same idea. We are all followers but we eventually all become leaders. How do we become leaders? God gave ministers to the church to train other ministers. Almost any local church can explode into growth when each member of the church recognizes that the church leadership exists to train them so that they develop in the basic ministerial functions and that as they develop they are called upon to develop others who will then develop others. Paul put it succinctly in II Timothy 2:2

> *"And the things that you have heard from me among many witnesses, commit these to faithful men who will be able to teach others also."*

The only requirement for each minister is that he be faithful, and that he teaches others as well. Therefore, the only people in the body of Christ who exclude themselves from the discipleship cycle are the unfaithful. Spiritual reproduction and multiplication are for faithful Christians. According to these words, God declares any Christian that excludes himself from this mandate unfaithful. There is honestly no other way to interpret the rejection of this responsibility and task.

Now let us suppose that you are part of a church of 100 members. Your pastor decides to spend the majority of his time working with 10 of the most mature people of the congregation. As he meets with this group, he teaches each one of them some basic lessons in pastoral ministry. Then he advances and begins to establish a spiritual mentoring relationship (discipleship) with each of these members and eventually is able to develop them as his own spiritual children as Paul did with Timothy and other younger brothers. Then he challenges each of the ten to lead a group of eight or nine members of the church passing on to them what he had taught each one of them in the same mentorship type fashion. He constantly reminds them that the purpose of these groups is to grow and multiply through evangelism and discipleship.

Then he challenges each one of them to win one new person to Christ each year and father that person on to spiritual maturity. If each person in this structure was successful in fulfilling this challenge, then the church would double its membership once a year and if it was able to sustain this multiplication over several years, it could win the entire world population in less than 28 years.

A congregation of 100 could win 12.8 billion converts in 28 years if each member in each generation would win one person each year and train the person to repeat the process. Just think what that would mean to you as a member of this church. God could use you to bring over a 128 million Disciples of Christ into His eternal arms in 28 generations of disciples! You would have the privilege of occasioning 128 million joy fests in heaven over a 28-year period!

Of course for this to happen there has to be a proper transmission of the vision and commitment to sustain each generation of disciples along with a number of other necessary details but the point of this chapter is to paint in broad strokes the vision of a spiritual inheritance that you can begin to build today.

Even if you accomplish just a fraction of the above example, you can expect to produce hundreds and thousands of spiritual children that will one day be your crown and glory in the Kingdom of Jesus the King of Kings.

CHAPTER 10

THE KINGDOM PARABLES OF MATTHEW 13

To many people, Matthew 13 is a mysterious chapter because it is full of parables commonly interpreted without a great amount of confidence, certainty and convincing cross-references with other Scripture passages. The seven parables in this chapter illustrate spiritual realities of the kingdom of heaven. God wants His people to understand these realities clearly. Again, it is important to recognize that the Gospel according to Matthew does not talk about salvation. The theme of the Gospel according to John is salvation, but the theme of Matthew is the dynamics of the kingdom of heaven. We must take care not to impose our own ideas or preconceived notions on any book chapter or reference of the Bible. These parables talk about the dynamics of the kingdom of heaven.

We can observe that the kingdom of heaven involves three aspects: the appearance of the kingdom of heaven, the reality of the kingdom of heaven and the physical and geopolitical manifestation of the kingdom of heaven. This final aspect corresponds to the 1000 year reign of Christ called the Millennium in which Jesus Christ, the King of Kings, will reign over the entire world from the city of Jerusalem, and Christians who overcome will reign with Him.

These seven parables, like many groups of seven in the Bible, are separated into two sub groups. The first four parables talk about the appearance of the kingdom of heaven, they begin with the phrase "the kingdom of heaven is like..." In these four parables, the intent is not to define explicitly every aspect of the kingdom, but to describe aspects of what appears to be the kingdom of heaven. The purpose of these parables is to warn against things that "appear" to be the kingdom of heaven but in reality, are not.

After Jesus told the parable of the sower recorded in Matthew chapter 13:3-8, His disciples asked Him why He spoke to the people in parables, He responded to their inquiry by giving them an explicit explanation of why He spoke through parables.

In verse 11, He explained that the reason for the parables was that His disciples were privileged to know the mysteries of the kingdom of heaven but this privilege was not extended to everyone in the multitude. Once again, it is important that we recognize that Jesus used explicit terminology whenever He spoke to His disciples. He taught in parables explicitly because He was not willing to reveal the mysteries of the kingdom of heaven to all people, only to His disciples. Scripture affirms that God's will is that none perish, but that all come to repentance and to the knowledge of the Father's will. Scripture also affirms that God's will is that all men be filled with the knowledge and revelation of all of His Word. However, because of the state of the majority of men's hearts, they have not been given the privilege of knowing the "mysteries of the kingdom of heaven". This touches on a general principle of receiving God's Word which determines that in order to understand God's will we must have an open and inquisitive heart and humbly receive it as fertile soil receives a seed. Jesus beautifully illustrated this principle in His first parable when He spoke of how each different type of soil receives seed.

We can be sure that Jesus definitely did not want to prevent anyone from being saved and that the meaning of these parables was not hidden to prevent people from recognizing their need for salvation and coming to repentance. Such is clearly not God's heart and neither is it the heart of Christ. It is easy to discern that the message concealed in these parables was not concerning salvation since there is no reference to the cross, to a savior, or was there any evangelistic appeal. Instead, the themes of these parables point to fruitfulness, true and false believers, things that appear to be the kingdom of heaven but are devoid of its true nature and different aspects of what happens in the kingdom of heaven. None of these parables elicited conversion and apparently Jesus spoke them to test the hearts of the hearers.

It is necessary to recognize that the term "mysteries of the kingdom of heaven" is a highly distinct term that does not indicate a general knowledge of God or of His Word. Jesus did not tell His disciples that they had received the privilege of knowing the Word of God, or the will of God, or even about the kingdom of God. He made it clear, that the knowledge of the mysteries (from the Greek *musterion*: a hidden or secret thing or something not obvious to the understanding) were revealed only to them as His disciples after having been initiated to exclusive privileges, one of which, is the special knowledge of the mysteries of the kingdom of heaven.

The Greek word *musterion* is used 27 times in the New Testament and is translated as mystery 22 times and mysteries 5 times. If you study the use of each instance, you will notice that it usually refers to several different mysteries of God, His Word and His work. It refers to the kingdom of heaven, the kingdom of God, to the grafting of the church into Israel, to marriage as a metaphor of Christ and the Church, to Babylon, and the woman and the great beast that carried her, to mention just a few. Therefore, we can easily conclude that the "mysteries" mentioned in the New Testament do not all refer to the same thing. For this reason, in order to discern which mystery each text is referring to, we must consider its context.

The mysteries of the kingdom of heaven that Christ was referring to were hidden in the parables of the kingdom of heaven that are recorded in Matthew 13 as well as several of the remaining chapters of Matthew's gospel account. As was mentioned previously, the kingdom of heaven is a term used exclusively in Matthew's account and refers to the Millennial Reign of Christ subsequent to the rapture and great tribulation and before Armageddon and the eternal state of Heaven. Once again, this is not common knowledge among most Christians and continues to remain almost a universal mystery.

After Jesus explained to His disciples that only to them was the privilege given of knowing the mysteries of the kingdom of heaven, He reiterated and expanded upon the subject for what amounted to several more paragraphs of the Biblical text.

In verse 12 He taught that in relation to this knowledge, whoever had it would receive more and with abundance. However, whoever did not have the knowledge of the mysteries of the kingdom of heaven would lose the little that they did have. Even a small amount of knowledge concerning the kingdom that they managed to accumulate, would be taken from them.

In verse 13, Jesus taught that since the multitude that heard His words had not been granted this knowledge, He spoke in parables because even though they had eyes and ears, they had no spiritual sight or sense of hearing. Then He cited the prophet Isaiah who prophesied that since His people had such dull spiritual eyes, ears and hearts in relation to His message, the judgment pronounced over them would be that they would not understand and repent, and thus would lose the chance to receive His healing. Since they had no propensity to turn, they were also denied the chance to turn.

This is a very serious condition, and tragically common among God's people. Note that Jesus related this to Isaiah's prophecy to God's people. God's did not direct these words to another nation; He spoke them to Israel, His own people. In the same way, Jesus did not direct the words in these verses to lost people but to those who were "children of Abraham" God's covenant people. Many Christians have ears but do not hear and eyes but do not see! Because of the dullness of their spiritual faculties, they lose any revelation that they might have previously had. This is a terrible indictment against God's people!

Then Jesus reassured His disciples and affirmed that such was not the case with them. They would be blessed because they had both spiritual sight and hearing to receive the explanation that He gave them privately. Then before explaining the parable of the sower, He affirmed that many prophets and righteous men of old desired to see and hear what they were witnessing but never had the chance, but they had the privilege of this opportunity, thus they were blessed.

JESUS EXPLAINS THE PARABLE OF THE SOWER:

Although Jesus does not explicitly identify all of the characters and objects in the parable of the sower, from the explanation that He gave, we can conclude that the seed represents the "word of the kingdom". As stated before, this does not correspond to the general "Word of God", nor to the gospel, but specifically to the word concerning the kingdom of heaven.

The four different soils represent the condition of the heart of those who hear the message of the kingdom. Those who received seed by the wayside did not understand the word of the kingdom upon hearing it and as a result, the birds devoured the seed that was sown into them. Jesus interpreted the birds as representing "the wicked one".

Now if Jesus intended to teach through this parable how different people receive the gospel, it would lead to some problematic conclusions. Firstly, it would imply that the gospel is hard to understand. Yet, God did not make the gospel understandable only to the intelligent. On the contrary, the gospel is not complicated, and the simplest child can understand it. People may struggle with believing the gospel, but understanding it is not difficult. Secondly, it would imply that the evil one has the ability to steal the seed of the gospel message out of the hearts of those who have received it based on a lack of understanding. The bible does not teach that man receives salvation by understanding the gospel nor does it teach that he can lose it by lack of understanding.

We need to understand very little in order to receive the gospel. If someone understands that by breaking God's law man became a sinner, and God being a just judge must condemn all sin and only His own Son was sinless. If someone understands that God condemned Christ as the substitute for man and that He was crucified and rose again the third day and that by believing these facts man can receive forgiveness and be "born of God", it is sufficient for him to be saved. These facts may be difficult for some to believe, but they are not difficult to understand. Someone can even claim not to understand why God would do this or how He did it, but that is irrelevant, one can still understand what He claimed that He did. Therefore, understanding is a given and not an issue. Only belief is an issue for salvation.

Now, understanding the meaning and significance of the word of the kingdom is not as easy. That is why Jesus called it "the mysteries of the kingdom of heaven". Normal Christians with eyes and ears and a normal capacity of understanding are often confused with the subject of the kingdom. This lack of understanding has to do with a hardened heart very much like the wayside of the parable. Having a hardened heart is normal for human beings; it is part of our nature. As young people, we are pliable and easily influenced and we can adapt to new ideas and ways of thinking. As we grow older however, it is harder and harder to accept something contrary to that which we have always been taught. The human heart is like a concrete foundation. While the slab is freshly poured, there is time to mix and shift it around, but as it begins to harden it eventually gets to the point that the only way to change something is to use a jackhammer and break up the foundation.

This dynamic is a two edged sword. It can be good when children are taught correctly because they will almost never be deceived into exchanging their values that are now set in concrete. However, it is also highly negative when children are taught a lie. Children who are raised with atheistic ideas turn out to be atheists who pretty much will never arrive at a theistic position by using their intellect. Their atheism is set in concrete and they cannot think in any other way. Their only hope is to have an experience that contradicts their preconceived ideas so that they can think straight.

This type of thing happens to all of us. Your convictions, values and worldview are pretty much fixed and you will pretty much be stuck with the template that your rearing has provided for you. Even though you consider yourself an open-minded person, you are only open to what make sense to the scripting that you have integrated into your understanding throughout the years.

Many people who consider themselves open-minded are only so in areas where they have received no teaching that contradicts their internal concept of reality. For example some Christians, because they have never been correctly taught or have never studied the bible on their own, are willing and able to accept a plethora of bad doctrine because it doesn't conflict with any of their preconceived ideas.

Others have received teaching from the bible and have learned to study it on their own and have developed their biblical convictions to such an extent that even if provided with scripture contrary to their position they will not be able to understand its validity because it contradicts their established system of truth. Again, this difficulty is just part of being human. God made us this way and meant it to be a protection for us if we learn correct truth from the beginning.

However, there is hope for all of us. The scriptures counsel us to become as children in this aspect. The bible instructs us to humble ourselves and not to lean on our own understanding. The Holy Spirit inspired Solomon in the Proverbs to teach us to seek after wisdom and not to despise godly teaching. The wayside represents those hearts that are not open to some truths of the Word. I believe that the "mysteries of the kingdom of heaven" remain mysteries because most people reject them and thus having eyes and ears, they cannot see nor hear nor perceive the unlocking of these mysteries. It is however, something that God offers to anyone with a heart prepared to receive it.

The Lord then explained that the second soil corresponds to those who hear the word (which is the same word throughout the parable) and they immediately receive it with joy. There is no problem with understanding in this case. They not only understand the word, they also receive it with joy. The evil one is not able to devour the seed, which then takes root and begins to grow.

The problem is that soon after receiving the word, tribulation or persecution arises and the person stumbles because of it. The word translated as "stumbles" is *skandalizo*, which indicates a figurative stumbling or taking of offence, to cause a person to begin to distrust whom he ought to trust and obey. What happens is that while the person readily embraces the new revelation, he soon discovers that it brings some adverse consequences to his life, thus he becomes offended, and begins to reject the word because of the difficulty it brings. As in the first soil, no further consequences are mentioned and Jesus began to talk about the third soil in which the seed was sown.

The third soil corresponds to the person who hears the word of the kingdom, understands and accepts it, and it begins to take root in the heart, but instead of becoming offended because of hardship and persecution, its progress is choked off because of the heart's excessive love of the world and worldly interests and involvement. Here the word is accepted and received as in the previous case but not with so much joy. There is a lot going on in this type of person's life and the word of the kingdom cannot compete with so many contrary interests. In this example, the Lord elaborated on the consequence of the action of the thorns, which was that this person became unfruitful.

The fourth and last soil mentioned in this parable corresponds to the person whose heart is ripe for receiving the seed of the word of the kingdom. This person hears the word, understands it, receives it and because his heart is not hard, because he doesn't stumble at tribulation or persecution and because he has cleared the weeds of worldly interest from his life, his roots are able to establish depth and he is able to bear fruit. Some people in this case are able to bear 100 times what was sown into their lives, others, 60 times and others 30 times. This bearing fruit is the objective of the planting of the seeds.

In each case except for the last, no fruit was produced. In the first case, because there was no understanding, no root could establish itself and consequently no fruit could be produced. In the second and third cases, the seeds started to take root but the stones and the weeds cut off their growth and no fruit was produced. Only in the last case was the seed able to develop roots so that fruit was produced. One of the mysteries of the kingdom of heaven is fruit bearing, which corresponds to making disciples.

The great commission that Christ gave just before His ascension is the making of disciples. The greatest scandal since He gave that commission is that, for the most part, His church has opted to do many things other than making disciples. One of the mysteries of the kingdom of heaven is the need to multiply disciples.

THE PARABLE OF THE WHEAT AND TARES – MAT. 13:24-30; 36-43

The next parable that Jesus told was also one that He later explained to His disciples. The sower of the good seed is the Son of Man or in other words, Jesus sows the good seed in the field. The field represents the world, not the church. Jesus Himself gave this interpretation. The good seeds are the sons of the kingdom and the tares are the sons of the wicked one. The enemy that sowed the tares is the devil, the harvest occurs at the end of the age, and the angels are the reapers. Jesus divinely interpreted each one of these details, so there can be no doubt about what He intended that they represent here. Nevertheless, it is quite common for Christians to confuse these details.

One of these commonly overlooked details is that the field represents the world and not the church. Many Christians are not clear concerning this and imagine that Jesus was teaching that there will always be true and false Christians in the church and nothing should be done to take out the false Christians because that will only happen at the end of the age at the harvest.

I have heard pastors quip that we will all have three surprises in heaven. The first surprise is that we make it to heaven. The second surprise is that those who we thought would make it didn't. The third surprise is that those who we thought would never make it did make it. This humorous antidote betrays a basic ignorance of God's Word concerning both salvation and true and false Christianity. I will not even

WHY SHOULD I BE GOOD? SALVATION IS FREE!

try to deal with the first surprise since no one will be surprised about getting to heaven. It is true that many will be surprised that they did not make it to heaven but the opposite is not true. The second and third surprises reveal a lack of understanding in part because of a misunderstanding of this parable. The bible never affirms that there can be wheat and tares in the church. Tares are sown in the world by the enemy, among those who were sown by the Son of Man, in the world.

This parable teaches that among all of those in the world who claim to be Christians, some are true Christians and others are false Christians. Just as the tares are very similar to wheat when they are young plants, false Christians and true Christians are difficult to tell apart at early stages of their development. Most of us are worlds apart from the agricultural society in which the New Testament was written and we don't know much about wheat and tares, but there are some details that the people who heard the parable were aware of.

Wheat and tares are almost identical in appearance when the crop is developing, so it is not profitable to try to separate them at this stage. However as the wheat begins to mature it turns yellow and the heads of the wheat begin to droop because of the weight and density of the grain. The tares however remain erect and take on a dark aspect because the seeds are black, and are somewhat toxic. This could suggest that those who are really God's people bow before the light of His glory while those who are false brethren are stiff-necked, proud and insist on questioning the authority of the King.

It is possible to distinguish the wheat from the tares. We can tell the difference. Some contend that we cannot know the difference because we should not judge anyone so that we are not judged. Jesus however never taught that we should never judge. Jesus said in John 7:24 that we should not judge according to appearance but with righteous judgment. We should not judge the intentions of others since we cannot see the heart of others. However, we can see peoples fruit and the bible is clear that in the church, we can know a tree by its fruit; therefore, we should judge fruit in the church.

When Jesus called the Pharisees a brood of vipers, He was judging them by their fruit. Now when the tares are young they cannot be distinguished because they have not yet produced fruit. However, as they mature, both the wheat and tares can be distinguished because of their fruit. Therefore, within the church there is no need to tolerate tares. The reason is that Jesus said that the tares should not be removed from the world. However, in the church we should remove them.

In 1Corinthians 5:9-13 Paul wrote:

> I wrote to you in my epistle not to keep company with sexually immoral people. Yet I certainly did not mean with the sexually immoral people of this world, or with the covetous, or extortioners, or idolaters, since then you would need to go out of the world.
>
> But now I have written to you not to keep company with anyone named a brother, who is sexually immoral, or covetous, or an idolater, or a reviler, or a drunkard, or an extortioner --- not even to eat with such a person.
>
> For what have I to do with judging those also who are outside? Do you not judge those who are inside? However, those who are on the outside God will judge. Therefore, "put away from yourselves the evil person."

This means that in the church there must be no tares. Nevertheless, in the world, there are true and false Christians. In 2012, the Pew Forum on religion and life estimated that 78.4% of the American Population claim to be Christian. How many do you think are true Christians? There are people that claim to be Christians who believe in evolution, and that there is no hell, who practice witchcraft, who believe that all religions lead to God, who worship images and who believe in reincarnation. They all claim to be Christians. This is the appearance of the kingdom. On the outside, you may never know that these people hold such beliefs. If these people are outside your church, they are in the world and neither you nor I have a mandate to judge or remove them. God will deal with them through His angels at the end of the age.

History has shown that every time Christians rise to political power their tendency is to try to legislate morality and try to gather the tares out of the wheat just as Jesus warned not to do in this parable. The Catholic Church during the Holy Inquisition and even the protestant church at other periods tried to remove the tares from the world and ended up destroying wheat, true Christians, including some of the best. We do not judge those who are in the world. However, in the church we must evaluate everyone because we can know each tree by its fruit. The Lord does not want us to judge according to appearances, because appearances can be misleading. However, when we wait for the fruit then we have a legitimate basis for judging and evaluating because by their fruit we shall know them. When we identify tares in the church, then the Word instructs us to refrain from having fellowship with them. We should not sit down and have a meal with them, or travel or associate with those who produce fruit of an unregenerate person. The reason is that they have an appearance but they do not have the reality, or fruit of the true life of God. Jesus said that in the church we should put the evil person away from us.

There is a dichotomy revealed in this parable that many Christians commonly misunderstand. We can call it appearance vs. origin. This parable shows the aspect of the kingdom of heaven that deals with two seeds, two plants, and two crops.

The important thing is not so much your appearance or what you do, but from which seed you originate. God does not accept tares no matter how good they look. In the same manner, God is not primarily concerned with our appearance or our works. He is more concerned with us being of the right seed. The important thing is to be wheat. Now some kernels of wheat may not have as good of an appearance as some tares.

Some Christians do not have a very good appearance at all, but they are wheat and God accepts them. David was a man after God's own heart and God chose him to replace Saul who God rejected even though he was able to maintain a much better appearance than David did. Saul's reputation was not stained with adultery, lying and murder like David's was, yet David's heart was responsive to God and Saul's heart was not. Jacob was of the right seed but he had all kinds of character flaws.

This does not mean that God is indifferent to sin. His desire is that we respond to Him and permit Him to lead us into the process of sanctification. However, the point of the parable is that God begins with the correct seed and not correct behavior and good appearance.

Many people that claim to be Christians argue that the important thing is to be good, and to practice good works, because God sees our works and knows the good that we have done and He sees that we are not doing anything bad. However, the truth is that God does not look at or consider first what we do. He considers as first importance what kind of seed we have originated from. If you are a seed of tares, you are useless to God and He will not work in your life. God does not try to fix tares; they do not have the right nature. However, if you came from a grain of wheat, you may not even look much like a healthy head of wheat. You may look sickly and diseased, dried up and blighted but you are wheat and will be harvested as wheat, not as a tare.

So initially we should not be concerned with what we do but with what we are. Do not stumble over the need for good behavior. Good behavior is important but not foundational and does not come first. Good works, correct behavior, even correct doctrine built upon a wrong foundation are useless and have no appeal to God. The judgment alluded to in this parable is not based upon what we do or have done but upon what we are.

The tares will burn and the wheat will shine forth as the sun in the kingdom of the Father. The wheat have God as their father, the tares are the sons of the wicked one.

This parable unlocks the kingdom mystery that God identifies His people on the basis of their nature and not their appearance and that it is not our concern as God's people to discover who in the world is of God and who is not. However, in the local church atmosphere, we are required to discern the reality of the life of our fellow members and we must not tolerate the tares to be actively operating within our midst. We must identify them and put them out.

In each of these first four parables of Matthew 13 with the exception of the first (the sower) the parable is prefaced with the phrase "The kingdom of heaven is like. . ." this speaks of the appearance of the kingdom, not necessarily the reality of the kingdom. That is why Jesus called these teachings "mysteries of the kingdom" because people mistake the appearance with the reality. These parables are meant to shed light on what the kingdom appears to be but really is not. Again, the exception is the parable of the sower, which describes a true principle of how different hearers receive the kingdom.

THE PARABLES OF THE MUSTARD SEED AND LEAVEN – MAT. 13:31–33

These two parables again describe what the kingdom of heaven looks like or appears to be. The kingdom is not really a mustard seed sown into a field and it is not really leaven hidden in three measures but it appears as such. There are aspects of the kingdom in this parable but the parable is not defining what the kingdom is . . . only what it appears to be.

Historically, the interpretation of these two parables is that they speak of the beneficial influence of the gospel in society. So then, the gospel or the kingdom of heaven is this leaven and the bread dough is society. When the kingdom of heaven is introduced into society, it affects it and causes a change in it, just as leaven effects a change in the bread dough, or so they claim. In the parable of the mustard seed, they say that the kingdom of heaven is this mustard seed. It starts very small it becomes a large tree and the birds of heaven make their nests in its branches. The birds of the heavens are people who are troubled and weighted down with burdens and problems and land on the branches of the tree to receive comfort.

However, this is a wrong and false interpretation of the Word of God. These two parables do not speak of positive things they speak of negative things. In reality, the emphasis of the parable of the sower is also negative. Seed was lost by the wayside, was scorched by the rocky soil, and was choked out by the thorns. The parable of the wheat and the tares is also negative; it speaks of something that was sown into God's field. These last two of the first four parables are also negative. They speak of the contrast between what originally was God's purpose for the kingdom and what the kingdom had apparently become.

Mustard plants appear to be trees, but they are herbs that have taken on the form and appearance of a tree. A mustard plant can reach up to 8ft in height, which is a gross anomaly for an herb but not particularly big for a true tree. It is vital to note that if Jesus was merely trying to illustrate the disparity between the small beginnings of the gospel and its broad reach He chose a woefully inadequate example in the mustard plant.

The largest disparity between seed and ultimate adult plant is probably the Sequoia tree of the US western coast. This tree has a seed as small as any mustard seed, yet it can become the largest individual organism on the planet reaching heights of hundreds of feet. Huge trees do not typically come from or produce huge seeds. Several species of trees reach a height of more than 300 feet, but Jesus chose to use a mustard plant in this parable.

The mustard plant is an herb and the kingdom of heaven can be likened to an herb. Nevertheless, when the herb begins to reach proportions of a tree, then it is taking on an appearance that does not correspond to its nature. In this context, the kingdom of God is not supposed to be a tree, nor does it take on the dimensions of a tree. Christianity today is not universally recognized as being exclusively composed of Evangelical bible believing born again Christians. Christianity includes evangelicals, Protestants, Catholics, Greek orthodox, almost all principle religions with the exception of Islam, Hinduism and Buddhism. Christianity today can include an infinite number of names and denominations all of which claim to be Christian. However, the kingdom of heaven is not constituted by all of these groups. Can we be sure that all of these groups enjoy the reality of the kingdom?

It is important to recognize that in order to understand the Bible we need to consider the context. We can understand each text of the Bible through its context. If we want to know the meaning of the birds of heaven in this text, we need to consider the context. Here in Matthew chapter 13 there is another place that speaks of birds, in the parable of the sower in verses 4 and 19. Since the Lord himself interpreted the birds in verse 4 of chapter 13 as demons, then we also must conclude that the birds of heaven in verse 32 also represent demons. You may ask if it possible to have demons inside of the church. The answer is no, not inside of the true church, but while any church may have the appearance of a true church, not all churches are local bodies of Christ.

The fact is that there are all kinds of churches with all kinds of religions teaching and doctrines and some with differing prophets. All of them call themselves churches, but not all of them make up the body of Christ. Once again, this parable is speaking of the appearance of the kingdom of heaven, not the kingdom of heaven itself. If a group, denomination, or church does not claim Jesus Christ as Lord, nor hold to apostolic doctrine, then of course, this group is outside of Christ and therefore subject to demonic infestation.

These parables refer to the appearance of the kingdom; they do have some elements of the kingdom but not the reality of the kingdom. In the reality of the kingdom, there are no demons swooping down and stealing seed and there are no demons perched on its branches. These things happen in the world, within a context that appears to be the kingdom of heaven, and the purpose of these parables is to make that distinction. Churches that have demons operating within their doors really do exist and these include demons of deceit, confusion and sorcery. The reason why this can occur is that they are not churches of Christ they merely have the appearance of a church. They may have even begun as true churches, just as the mustard plant began as an herb and turned into a freak of nature taking on the form of a tree. The parable of the mustard seed speaks of degeneration. Jesus was explaining that the appearance of the kingdom of heaven is like an herb that degenerated, mutated, and became a tree.

Herbs must be planted periodically but trees are perennial and only need to be planted one time. In reality, the kingdom of heaven is like an herb that is constantly fed and nourished with the Word and the Spirit. However, when an herb becomes a tree, it becomes like a monument to itself and needs no outside care.

An herb has leaves but a tree has branches. An herb is smaller and is a single unit, but a tree constantly sprouts new branches and each branch branches into smaller branches and no longer forms a small unity but a giant network. Herbs do not have significant root systems while trees have extensive and deep root systems. In this context, deep roots represent something negative because it shows that a tree is deeply rooted in the world system, but herbs are much less attached to the world.

This parable shows the grave danger of the possibility of the church degenerating into something that is not of God. This is an alert for each denomination and each local church. Many churches in their desire to grow abandon the foundation of the pure Word of God. Many churches no longer want to preach the purity of the gospel.

The Parable of the Leaven in Three Measures

As we have said before, to understand any Bible text, we must consider its context. When this parable speaks of leaven, we must interpret what this symbol represents. Within the context of the whole Bible, we can easily demonstrate that leaven is never interpreted as something positive but rather something always negative, something evil. For example in Matthew 16:12, Jesus spoke of the doctrine of the Pharisees and the Sadducees and that the disciples should be careful of the hypocritical teachings of these men. In Matthew 16:6, Jesus told His disciples to be careful of the leaven of the Pharisees, the leaven of legalism, the leaven of hypocrisy, and the leaven of religiosity devoid of

God. In 1Corinthians 5:6 Paul encouraged the Corinthians to throw out the old leaven and bring in unleavened bread. In the Old Testament, the Lord prohibited the Jews from bringing an offering that had leaven in it. God does not accept leaven in any form and always describes it as something sinful and negative.

In the parable of the leaven, the woman put leaven in three measures of meal. Since we have determined that leaven is never something positive, we must conclude that this leaven does not symbolize the influence of the kingdom of heaven that grows in the world. This leaven has nothing to do with liturgy, style of music or dress. The enemy has placed this leaven in the church for the purpose of contamination. Too often believers tolerate the leaven of hypocrisy and sin within the church.

Many churches today pay no attention to sin in any practical way and no longer speak of it as something to be resisted and eliminated. Leaven symbolizes several things. Leaven symbolizes teaching and behavior. It symbolizes the attempt or intention to make the gospel lighter and more digestible. Unleavened bread is heavy, dense, harder to chew, while leavened bread is light, full of air and almost melts in one's mouth. Leaven in the church symbolizes the attitude that the Word of God must be made more palatable and easier to assimilate.

Many churches feel that too many things in the Bible are overly polemic to be preached in their pulpits. In many churches, there is a reluctance to preach about sacrifice, the need for sacrificial giving of money, time and energy. Freedom is preached to the detriment of service. Hell is another subject that many churches avoid. Many preachers and teachers feel that the subject of hell unwarrantably startles and frightens potential hearers of the gospel. In many pulpits all over the world, the theme of judgment is never dealt with.

While it is true that there is no more condemnation for those who are in Christ Jesus, the Bible clearly teaches that God will judge the living and the dead. There will be a judgment of God's people and a judgment of those who do not know God. Instead of these weightier matters, churches prefer to emphasize more agreeable subjects like prosperity, blessing, healing, relationships, and other things that interest the majority of people today. The thinking is that if people come to church services and have to listen to difficult subjects calling for sacrifice, warning of judgment, pressuring for change, that they won't come back.

The argument is that avoidance of these themes is one of the strategies for winning people over. It is born from the conviction that we cannot preach everything to everybody, only what the people are prepared to hear. After all, they are just children and can only eat baby food. However, all of these attitudes and lines of thinking only serve to contaminate the work of God. They contribute to producing a light and shallow Christianity full of leaven. Leavened bread is easy to eat but has no consistency; it is sweet but not nutritious.

Many groups that espouse these ideas are churches; they are wheat, true bread dough, but the leaven of sin and world has entered into the lump. We should not be concerned if the lump is dense and hard at times. Several times in the gospels, we read of people telling Jesus that His teaching and His sayings were hard. Many people observe that Jesus taught with authority and with grace, unlike the scribes and the Pharisees, but others also said that His sayings were hard and difficult. Many times the Word of God is like unleavened bread: difficult to chew, neither as pleasant to eat nor as easy to digest, but much more nourishing.

God does not accept leaven, which in reality is nothing but the decomposition of a lump of dough through the multiplication of bacteria. The action of leaven is really a rotting process, and God rejects this rotting process. God rejects the rot of legalism, but He also rejects the rot of liberalism. Jesus Christ is preparing His bride, which is the true church, to be spotless and blameless.

The church is full of the leaven of divorce, tolerance of homosexuality and tolerance of sin in influential members in the church because of their social or financial status. Leaven speaks of the rottenness of preachers and teachers who no longer preach the Word of God, but their own opinions. Leaven speaks of the rottenness of the fear of saying what needs to be said because someone may turn their back and leave the church. Leaven speaks of the rottenness of a man-focused agenda that is valued more than the Holy Spirit inspired model of the Scriptures that teach that the church belongs to Jesus Christ and His Holy Spirit is the one that gives direction for its own edification.

We can easily interpret the details of the parable of the leaven with a basic knowledge of church history even though it is not common to do so. Without stretching the metaphors in this parable to fit any preconceived interpretations, the three measures of leavened meal correspond to the three main branches of Christianity, which are Roman Catholicism, Eastern Orthodox Christianity, and Protestantism. The woman points to Jezebel mentioned in John's letter to the church in Thyatira, which is the fourth of the seven letters just as this is the fourth of the seven parables of Matthew 13. According to history, Thyatira represents the apostate Roman Catholic Church from which the other two divisions appeared, thus Jesus spoke of a woman who hid three measures of leavened meal.

As we have previously demonstrated, the bible never references leaven in in a positive way. It always represents sin, corruption, and something necessary to eliminate. The scriptures repeatedly call for unleavened bread. Jesus warned the disciples about the leaven of the Pharisees. Since leaven represents something negative in all other places in the bible it would make no sense for Jesus to use it as a positive example here.

Bakers use leaven in making bread so that it is easier to eat. The leaven contains contaminating bacteria that change the consistency of the wheat flour. Unleavened bread is heavy, dense, and harder to eat than fluffy and light leavened bread. In the same way, large portions of the church have concluded that parts of God's Word and His kingdom principles are too heavy and need to be leavened to make them lighter and easier to bear.

Leaven also affects the dough in the sense that it inflates it to a greater size while compromising its consistency. I believe that all Christians should strive to do everything within their means to contribute to the growth of the church of which they are a part. However, church growth is not the ultimate goal. It is a worthy and necessary goal but not the ultimate goal. God wants to see His church grow but not at the expense of compromising its true character.

In "the Vine", the church that I am part of, we do all kinds of things that some people could judge as compromising the message of the gospel. However, we do not compromise the gospel message and we do not refrain from preaching the weightier matters of the Christian life like, holiness, chastity, integrity, sacrifice, etc. However, we quite often do things that most churches would consider worldly, like dressing up as giant jelly beans and evangelizing people on the beach or at Christmas time dressing up like an army of Santa Clauses and using the occasion which is not even biblical and necessarily "spiritual" to reach the un-churched with the message of the Gospel. We "become all things to all men" in order to save some. However, this does not happen in most American churches where the preaching service is limited to one hour and the sermon never passes 20 minutes.

The themes in many of these churches are limited only to the attractive, crowd-pleasing messages like prosperity, success, healing, and deliverance. The thinking is that if churches preach the meat of the Word in their meetings that the masses will reject it and not give it a chance. However, the truth is that the masses have always rejected the biblical messages of holiness; sacrifice, Christian duty, and spiritual warfare. The greater part of God's people have always had a hard time with prophetic rebuke, repentance, godly discipline and sacrifice.

These two parables constitute a very serious warning for the church today. We do not want to be a piece of unleavened bread that no one eats. We do not want to be a dry and unpleasant church. We do not want to be the mustard seed that never falls into the good soil and never produces any fruit. However, we also do not want to be a mustard seed that degenerates into a giant herb that has lost its true qualities, nor do we want to be a fluffy lump of leaven bread devoid of any nourishing substance.

There is a logical sequence to these four parables. In the first parable, Jesus spoke about the sower of seed. We have seen that Jesus is the one who sowed the seed, and the seed is the word of the kingdom, the word of the kingdom is a specific message of the Word of God. Therefore, Jesus sows the seed, and the seed is the Word. However, in His explanation of the parable of the wheat and the tares in verses 37 and 38 He explains that the Son of Man sows the seeds, the field is the world, and the good seeds are the sons of the kingdom. There is an apparent difficulty in interpreting the seed.

In the first parable, the seed is the word, specifically the word of the kingdom. However, in the second parable the seeds are the sons of the kingdom. It is because of this difficulty that it is so important that we understand the metaphor of the seed, and this metaphor is part of the basis for the understanding the whole gospel.

The seed is the word, but in John chapter 1:1 it says "in the beginning was the Word, and the Word was with God, and the Word was God." Therefore, the seed is the word, but the word is also a person. The word is the Lord Jesus Christ.

In the original Greek, two words translate into the English "seed" *sporos* and *sperma*. *Sporos* is the seed of the plant kingdom normally used for sowing in a field and *sperma* is the seed of the animal kingdom. The word translated as seed in these passages is *sperma*. This is strange because a sower does not go into the field to sow animal seed. *Sporos* is seed for sowing not *sperma*. The modern reader easily overlooks this detail because Jesus's words were translated from another language. However, the people who were listening to Jesus speak through this parable obviously noticed that He changed the term. Although He spoke these first four parables as mysteries, this detail was a generous clue to the meaning of His words.

The seed is the word, the seed is a person, the Lord Jesus Christ, and the seed are the sons of the kingdom. The Bible says that we have been begotten by the Word because the Word is a seed. Each child of God was begotten and born of God when the seed of the Word was planted and took root in their hearts, and they received the very nature of God. When the seed of the Word of God enters your human spirit, you are born again and become a new creation. You become a child of God, because of the biblical principle that each species multiplies according to its kind. An apple seed begets apples, an orange seed begets oranges, and God's seed begets sons of God. The Lord sows eternal life within our human spirit, and eternal life is not just a life that lasts forever, it is the *Zoe* of God, or the quality and nature of the life of God.

So here, we see the sequence that in the first parable, the seed is the word of the kingdom, but in the second parable, the seeds are the sons of the kingdom. In the first parable, the sower himself is a seed, and He sows himself in the hearts of His hearers. When His hearers receive the seed within their hearts then they also become seeds, and they themselves can be sown to produce new seed. Then when the sons of the kingdom open their mouth and speak the Word, they sow themselves into the hearts of their hearers.

In the parable of the sower, the kingdom of heaven appears to be like each one of the soils described in the parable. However, the reality of the kingdom only happens when the seed of the kingdom is sown into the good soil and germinates to produce some thirty-fold some sixty-fold in some one-hundred-fold. The wayside, the rocky soil, and the thorny soil are merely appearances of the kingdom. The kingdom begins with the good soil after the seed of the kingdom has been sown in it.

The kingdom has a present and a future aspect. Today the kingdom is among us but it is a spiritual kingdom; it is real but we cannot directly perceive it with our physical senses. Jesus warned that when someone says the kingdom is here or the kingdom is there we should not pay attention because the kingdom is within us. The apostle Paul said that the kingdom is not meat and drink but justice, peace and joy in the spirit. However, in the future, the kingdom will be physical and everyone will see it

Jesus did not speak the last three parables of Matthew chapter 13 to the multitude but in a private setting with His disciples. In verse 36, we read, "Then Jesus sent the multitude away and went into the house. And His disciples came to Him, saying, 'Explain to us the parable of the tares of the field.'" Jesus spoke the first four parables from the boat on the beach of the sea, but He shared the next three parables privately to His disciples. This indicates that the meaning of these parables is different from the first four.

In the Bible, the number seven has a special meaning. Seven is the number of God; it is the number of completion. We must not imagine that the number of parables in this chapter is without significance. There are several examples in the Bible of groupings of seven, for example; in Revelation, there are the seven churches, the seven seals, the seven trumpets, and the seven bowls, and several other arrangements of groups of seven. Typically, each grouping of seven is further defined in groups of 6+1, 3+4, or 4+3. In Matthew chapter 13, the first four parables form one group, and speak of the appearance of the kingdom, and the last three parables form a second group and illustrate another aspect of the kingdom of heaven.

THE PARABLE OF THE HIDDEN TREASURE - MATTHEW 13:44

"Again, the kingdom of heaven is like treasure hidden in a field, which a man found and hid; and for joy over it He goes and sells everything that He has and buys that field."

This parable is popularly interpreted by placing the gospel as the hidden treasure, the man that found and hid the treasure represents people that seek out and come to the gospel, and when they find it, they abandon everything and buy it to secure their salvation. The problem with this interpretation is that it contradicts the message of the gospel. In the first place, no one can buy salvation, because salvation is a gift given on the basis of grace.

> *"For by grace you have been saved through faith, and that not of yourselves; it is the gift of God, not of works, lest anyone should boast." (Ephesians 2:8, 9)*

No one can purchase salvation; therefore, we must reject this interpretation. The correct interpretation according to the Scriptures is that the hidden treasure is the church and the field is the world. Since the church is composed of God's people, then we can also say that this treasure represents the children of the kingdom. If you are born again, you are this treasure and the man that found you is the Lord Jesus, He found you in the field, which represents the world.

Jesus did not give the interpretation of this parable but the rest of Scripture reveals the meaning of it. First, we can ask how this man knew that this hidden treasure was in the field. The parable says that it was a hidden treasure. When we think of hidden treasure, we usually think of a chest buried in the earth. Unless we understand certain background history from the Old Testament and certain Jewish laws regarding the transfer of property, the details of this parable will indeed remain mysterious.

Imagine if you and I were Jews in Old Testament times and I sold you a plot of land. If after a number of years you decided to sell the plot of land to someone else, I would have the first legal option of buying back the property that was originally mine. This process of acquiring a previously owned piece of property was called redemption. Whoever owned a piece of property which at one point was sold, whenever that same piece of property was once again placed on the market, the original owner had the right by law to redeem that which he had previously owned. If I decided that I was not interested in purchasing the land back from you, then you would be free to sell it to whomever you wish.

The Bible explicitly claims that the earth belongs to the Lord, and in three separate passages the words: "the earth is the LORD's, and all its fullness." affirm this fact. In spite of the fact that Satan has become the lord of the worldly system, and that "the whole world lies under the sway of the wicked one." The earth belongs to God. It has always belonged to God. In the beginning, in the first chapter of Genesis we have the account of when God turned over the earth to the man that He had created. Through man's sin and disobedience, he effectively yielded control of the earth to Satan and since that time, Satan has been the god of this world.

When Christ went to the cross, He effectively paid the price to redeem the earth that man had turned over to the devil through his sin. The detail in the parable that the treasure was hidden can be interpreted as Satan's failure to recognize the value of God's people. Satan's only concern was taking what belonged to God, and ruling over and controlling the earth. The treasure was "hidden" because the evil one was unable to discern the value of what was on the earth. However, God saw its value.

THE PARABLE OF THE PEARL OF GREAT PRICE - MATTHEW 13:45–46

> *"Again, the kingdom of heaven is like a merchant seeking beautiful pearls, who, when he had found one pearl of great price, went and sold all that he had and bought it."*

The formation of a pearl is seemingly a miraculous event. Unlike precious stones that must be mined from the earth, live oysters far below the surface of the sea form pearls. Precious stones must be cut and polished to bring out their beauty. However, pearls need no such treatment to reveal their beauty. They are completely formed as finished products right out of the oysters possessing a shimmering iridescence and luster and soft inner glow unlike any other gem on earth.

A natural pearl begins its formation as a foreign object, usually a parasite or piece of shell broken by the entrance of a parasite that eats its way into and lodges itself in an oyster's soft inner body where it cannot be expelled. To ease this irritant, the oyster's body takes defensive action. The oyster begins to secrete a substance that becomes smooth, hard and crystalline around the irritant in order to protect itself. This substance is called "nacre." As long as the irritant remains within its body, the oyster will continue to secrete nacre around it, layer upon layer. Over time, the silky crystalline coatings will completely encase the irritant. The result, ultimately, is the lovely and lustrous gem called a pearl.

How something so wondrous emerges from an oyster's way of protecting itself is one of nature's loveliest surprises. For the nacre is not just a soothing substance. It is composed of microscopic crystals of calcium carbonate, aligned perfectly with one another, so that light rays passing along the axis of one crystal reflect and refract to produce a rainbow of light and color. Each pearl is a mixture of mineral and animal substances. Humankind is analogous to the nature of pearls in that we were created from the dust of the earth receiving the breath of God and subsisting as the highest form of animal life.

This parable and the parable of the hidden treasure do not speak of the appearance of the kingdom of heaven. These two parables refer to the great value that God places on His people who are the sons of the kingdom. According to the factors that determine value, God considers us precious because of His great desire for us, much like economic principles of supply and demand (we are in short supply and great demand), rarity, condition, individuality, and great significance.

THE PARABLE OF THE DRAGNET - MATTHEW 13:47-51

"Again, the kingdom of heaven is like a dragnet that was cast into the sea and gathered some of every kind, which, when it was full, they drew to shore; and they sat down and gathered the good into vessels, but threw the bad away. So it will be at the end of the age. The angels will come forth, separate the wicked from among the just, and cast them into the furnace of fire. There will be wailing and gnashing of teeth."

Frequently the interpretation given to this parable is pretty much the same as that of the parable of the wheat and tares. The symbol of the dragnet is interpreted as meaning the gospel or the church that is thrown into the sea, which represents the world, so all kinds of fish are brought into the church. There are good fish, bad fish, and all kinds of fish that represent the different people that come into the church. Then at the end of the age, the Angels will come and separate the good fish from the bad. This is the common interpretation but it does not correlate with the order of things in Scripture. This parable refers to a very specific moment in church history. The dragnet is not a symbol of the gospel of grace but of what the book of Revelation calls "the eternal gospel."

In Revelation chapter 14:6, 7 we read

> *"Then I saw another angel flying in the midst of heaven, having the everlasting gospel to preach to those who dwell on the earth --- to every nation, tribe, tongue, and people --- saying with a loud voice, "Fear God and give glory to Him, for the hour of His judgment has come; and worship Him who made heaven and earth, the sea and springs of water."*

The parable of the dragnet refers to the end of the age. The Bible teaches that one day Satan will raise up a man called the Antichrist. This does not mean necessarily that his name or title will be the Antichrist, but he will be anti or against Christ. The Antichrist will make a covenant with the nation of Israel for a period of seven years. During the first 3 1/2 years, he will respect this covenant and then he will break it. At this time, he will demand that all people worship him, and he will persecute the Jews and all those Christians that are alive on the earth at that time.

There is a distinct difference between the rapture when Christ comes to reap His first fruits, those who love His appearing, who have washed their garments, and were prepared for the bridegroom just before the great tribulation and the second coming of Christ which will occur at the end of the great tribulation. A great persecution will arise because of the mark that the Antichrist will require everyone to receive on the forehead or right-hand. Both the Jews and the Christians on the earth at that the time will refuse to receive this mark and as a result, they will suffer persecution. They will not be able to buy or sell and for the most part will be excluded from the economy of the world at that time. They will go through a very difficult time during the last three and a half years of this covenant.

After this, Jesus will return a second time descending upon the Mount of Olives to set up His earthly kingdom. When He returns the Bible says in second Timothy 4:1 that He will judge the living and the dead. There will be two judgments, the judgment of the living and the judgment of the dead. The dead will be resurrected in two distinct occasions.

When Jesus returns the second time, all the dead in Christ will be resurrected and judged. The bible calls this judgment the judgment seat of Christ or the bema seat. This judgment is only for the children of

God, those who are saved. This judgment has nothing to do with hell or damnation; it is a judgment to determine rewards and discipline. At the end of the Millennium, those who have died without Christ will be resurrected and judged but it will be a judgment of condemnation and damnation.

When Jesus returns at the end of the great tribulation there will still be many people alive on the earth and the different nations will continue to exist. There will also be a judgment for those who are still alive after the great tribulation.

Jesus referred to this group of people as "the nations", those people that had managed to survive the great tribulation but had not yet converted to the Lord. This judgment called "the judgment of the nations" will be exclusive to this specific period: after the tribulation and before the Millennium. Therefore, the dragnet of this parable refers to the eternal gospel that was cast into the sea. The sea is a symbol of death. Christians are no longer in the sea, so none of the fish referred to in this parable are Christians they are all unsaved. When we study this parable, we should also consider chapter 25 of Matthew where Jesus talks about the judgment of the nations.

THE SON OF MAN WILL JUDGE THE NATIONS – MATTHEW 25:31- 46

"When the Son of Man comes in His glory, and all the holy angels with Him, then He will sit on the throne of His glory. All the nations will be gathered before Him, and He will separate them one from another, as a shepherd divides His sheep from the goats.

And He will set the sheep on His right hand, but the goats on the left. Then the King will say to those on His right hand, 'Come, you blessed of My Father, inherit the kingdom prepared for you from the foundation of the world: for I was hungry and you gave Me food; I was thirsty and you gave Me drink; I was a stranger and you took Me in; I was naked and you clothed Me; I was sick and you visited Me; I was in prison and you came to Me.'

Notice this is the second coming of Christ, which occurs after the rapture and at the end of the great tribulation. Instead of a secret coming, as a thief, this is His coming in glory at the time when He will set up his earthly millennial rule and sit on His throne in Jerusalem. All the citizens of nations that have survived the destruction and disasters of the great tribulation will gather before Him and He will separate them as a shepherd separates sheep from the goats. Goats, while not exactly depicted in the bible as evil, do have a less meek nature than sheep do, they are also not as easy to lead, and are more independent and mischievous. Notice what He tells those who He calls sheep that He separates on His right side: "Come, blessed of My Father," He did not say "blessed of your Father," This indicates that His Father was not necessarily their Father. The basis for the two separate and contrasting destinies of these people was how they treated the Son of Man when He was hungry, thirsty, alone, without clothing, sick and in prison.

> *"Then the righteous will answer Him, saying, 'Lord, when did we see you hungry and feed You, or thirsty and give You drink? When did we see You a stranger and take You in, or naked and clothe You? Or when did we see You sick, or in prison, and come to You?'*
>
> *And the King will answer and say to them, 'Assuredly, I say to you, inasmuch as you did it to one of the least of these My brethren, you did it to Me.'*
>
> *"Then He will also say to those on the left hand, 'Depart from Me, you cursed, into the everlasting fire prepared for the devil and his angels: for I was hungry and you gave Me no food; I was thirsty and you gave Me no drink; I was a stranger and you did not take Me in, naked and you did not clothe Me, sick and in prison and you did not visit Me.'*
>
> *"Then they also will answer Him, saying, 'Lord, when did we see You hungry or thirsty or a stranger or naked or sick or in prison, and did not minister to You?' Then He will answer them, saying, 'Assuredly, I say to you, inasmuch as you did not do it to one of the least of these, you did not do it to Me.' And these will go away into everlasting punishment, but the righteous into eternal life."*

Neither one of these groups knew that they were dealing with the Son of Man. Jesus explains that their treatment of the least of His brethren was equated with their treatment of Him. These least of His brethren were the Christians that were left behind on the earth at the rapture and also the Jews. The Christians that remained were the spiritual brethren of Christ and the Jews were His natural brothers. Those who the Son of

Man will place to His right, who are called "sheep" and "righteous", are the unconverted people alive on the earth during the great tribulation who will not receive the mark of the beast and who will help others who have not received it. They will give them food and drink, housing and clothes. When they are imprisoned and sick, will help them and visit them. Those on the left, who were called goats, are simply people who managed to survive the great tribulation by accepting the mark of the beast and had offered no help to those who had not received the mark, their destiny will be destruction in the fire. The ones on the right will be those who will enter into Christ's millennial kingdom, which will be a tremendous blessing.

In this kingdom described in these verses those who are qualified as over comers will reign with Christ, the believing Jews will be the priests, and those who have been separated as the good fish, and the sheep, will be the subjects of the kingdom.

THE EXAMPLE OF THE HOUSEHOLDER - MATTHEW 13:51-52

Jesus said to them, "Have you understood all these things?" They said to Him, "Yes, Lord." Then He said to them, "Therefore every scribe instructed concerning the kingdom of heaven is like a householder who brings out of his treasure things new and old."

In order to properly interpret these two verses that conclude Christ's teaching on the kingdom of heaven through the seven parables it is necessary to understand the implications of the two terms "scribe" and "householder" and consider these words in the context of the message of the parables.

Strong's Greek dictionary defines the meaning and function of a scribe in the Bible as a man learned in the Mosaic Law and in the sacred writings, an interpreter and teacher. Scribes examined the more difficult and subtle questions of the law. Unfortunately, to the detriment of biblical truth, they often added to the Mosaic Law and made decisions of various kinds thought to better explain its meaning and scope. Since the advice of men skilled in the law was needed in the examination in the causes and the solution of the difficult questions, they were enrolled in the Sanhedrin; and are mentioned in connection with the priests and elders.

The word Householder, *oikodespotes* in the original Greek from *oikos* (house or household) and *despotes* (lord or ruler), is the term used for the head of a household or circle of close relationships. The word "house" or "household" from the Greek *oikos* was used in Acts 11 and 16 when salvation was offered to Cornelius and to the Philippian jailer and their house or household. The idea that this term represents is the social circle that each of these two men represented. This means that the term householder refers to men who were the recognized leaders and influencers over a group of extended family members and close-knit friends and relatives. In terms that are more modern, we could call such individuals "house church leaders".

With the understanding of these two terms, we can properly interpret what Jesus concluded as He debriefed his disciples on the subject of the kingdom of heaven. First, He made sure that they understood the messages that He meant to transmit through each one of the parables. Then He applied the dissemination of this message to each of His disciples, training them as scribes or interpreters and teachers that would speak of these mysterious and veiled truths to each of their perspective circles of influence.

Jesus was strategically training His disciples to spread the gospel of the kingdom among His people. Each of them through the knowledge of the secrets that He was teaching them (things new) and their knowledge of Old Testament truth (things old) would be able to instruct the members of their corresponding household (circle of influence) in how to rightly divide the Word of Truth. In accomplishing this they would be able to avoid the spiritual confusion and myopia that has permitted the degeneration of genuine and legitimate moves of God into spiritually lifeless bodies of religious hypocrisy that have choked out the true move of God and as a result have needlessly delayed His coming.

OVERVIEW OF WHAT THE HOUSEHOLDERS SHOULD TEACH:

Jesus taught through the parable of the sower that only a prepared heart that has not been hardened with the constant traffic of worldly activities, that is not filled with stones of stumbling at hardships for the sake of the gospel, that has not succumbed to the thorns of worldly pleasures and attractions can receive the Word of the kingdom. When this Word is sown into a prepared heart, it will take root and produce fruit some one hundred-fold, some sixty-fold and some thirty-fold. This is not a question of spiritual life vs. death or of salvation vs. damnation, but of spiritual sterility vs. fruitfulness. Many have the appearance of the kingdom but only those who are spiritually reproductive possess the reality of the kingdom.

Through the parable of the wheat and tares, He taught another negative aspect of the appearance of the kingdom; the principle that teaches that appearances are not foundational but nature is foundational. Satan is the spiritual father of those compared to tares and as such, no matter how good of an appearance they are able to maintain, they are fundamentally disqualified to serve in God's kingdom. In contrast the kernels of wheat represent God's people and even though they may not have a better appearance than tares, because of their nature (that of wheat) they are qualified to participate in God's kingdom.

Through the parable of the mustard seed, Christ taught that size does not matter. Church growth never "proves" that the expansion is due to the blessing of God. While He did not imply that the church should avoid growth, the lesson is that a true move of God can be contaminated and become deeply rooted in the world's systems of values and grow in a degenerate way that eventually attracts religious demonic spirits.

In the parable of the leaven, which is the last of the first group of four parables, Christ taught of the danger of the true move of God degenerating through the leaven of sin. This malignant influence causes the expansion of numerical and financial growth and power in such a way that while more attractive to the masses, it has lost its nutritional elements of spiritual edification. It causes the move of God to be watered down and diluted in such a manner that a dynamic and spiritually powerful move of God is reduced to a giant but spiritually impotent human organization.

In the parables of the hidden treasure and the pearl of great price, the Lord revealed the value of His people. While it is true that without Christ we can do nothing, and as the Apostle Paul was well aware of that He was the chief of sinners, and as Isaiah lamented that he was unclean before the presence of God, in this sense we are nothing and can do nothing. However, in God's perspective, we are precious and even though our value is due to Him and His investment, it is a spiritual reality and something necessary to recognize. We have value because God the Father gave us value and has invested His resources in us to extend His influence throughout the earth. The way that He spreads this influence is through the gospel of the kingdom. While the gospel of grace produces converts, the gospel of the kingdom produces "householders" or spiritual fathers who disciple the members of their circle of influence in order to multiply their own influence. This kingdom reality (as opposed to kingdom appearance) causes the growth of the true kingdom of heaven.

In the final parable of the dragnet, the Lord clears up any confusion about who will be ushered into the kingdom of heaven. The manifestation of the kingdom of heaven which is the final aspect of the kingdom will begin with and include all of those people that survive the ravages of the great tribulation that denied receiving the mark of the beast and were kind to the "least of Christ's brethren" (the believing Jews and Christians that were unprepared for the rapture). This group of people will be ruled by Christ and His ministers composed of Old and New Testament saints that have been resurrected and qualified to reign with Christ through His judgment seat (the Judgment seat of Christ, or the Bema seat).

I will ask you one final time, If salvation is by faith, if it is free, why bother being good or holy? My prayer is that you consider the scriptures and interpretations offered in this book and search the scriptures to see if perhaps you have held an incomplete view of this subject. My prayer is that having spiritual eyes and ears you are able to use them to see and hear what the Spirit is saying to the churches. God bless you!

> *"And he who overcomes, and keeps My works until the end, to him I will give power over the nations "He shall rule them with a rod of iron" Revelation 2:26-27a*

If this book has been a blessing to you please help promote it by leaving a favorable reveiw on amazon.com. This will help it gain more visibility when people browse the site. You can do so by visiting:

http://www.amazon.com/should-good-Salvation-free-ebook/dp/B009I3TNZ8

Then just hit the button that says: "**Write a customer review**" like the one below.

5 star		3	Share your thoughts with other customers
4 star		1	**Write a customer review**
3 star		0	

ABOUT THE AUTHOR

In December of 1983, Rick was sent as a missionary to Brazil to work with an organization called Project Amazon. He worked in a boat factory as manager and factory supervisor and oversaw the construction of over 40 houseboats, 1 yacht, and a Catamaran Hospital boat for church planting use along the Amazon River.

He married his wife Sandra who is a Brazilian national in July of 1985 and they assumed the pastorate of one of the Project Amazon churches in 1988. In 1990, Rick and his wife were sent as church planters to the state of Amapá, where they planted three churches for Project Amazon.

In 2008, they affiliated themselves with the Vine International and the last church that they planted became one of the Churches under the care of this organization.

In December of 2009, they were invited to join a church planting endeavor in Southern Florida. They accepted the invitation and turned the last church in Brazil over to the Brazilian Nationals in March of 2010.

In late 2011 they made the move to Southern Florida where they currently reside. Rick's family is bilingual and they have been serving with the Vine Florida which began as a Brazilian church. In 2013, they began overseeing the English ministry while the Brazilian ministry continues to flourish.

In Brazil, Rick has written extensively in the Portuguese language in the area of Christian worker training. He has written Bible study guides, evangelistic tracts, and hundreds of small group lesson guides. From June 2009-2010 he hosted a highly successful Christian radio program with his wife called "Overcomers on the air".

Rick maintains a Facebook page with a little over 1,850 fans called "Why be Holy if Salvation is by Grace" where he has posted hundreds of short, pithy phrases and where he has published several articles in the notes section. http://www.facebook.com/why.be.holy

Rick is also the creator and administrator of www.Vinebrancher.com a blog with articles to edify your Christian walk as an overcomer.

Also you can visit Rick's Amazon Author's page at:

http://www.amazon.com/Richard-Lee-Spinos/e/B00A911TZK

The Vine Florida's Facebook page:

http://www.facebook.com/TheVineFlorida

The Vine Florida's church website:

http://www.thevineusa.org

Rick's LinkedIn profile:

http://www.linkedin.com/pub/richard-spinos/62/44a/217

Rick's Twitter account:

http://twitter.com/Rick_Spinos

On the next few pages you will find the basic materials that are used by the Vine International to edify new converts and train them to be responsible members of the local church and overcomers qualified to reign with Christ when He comes to set up His glorious Kingdom.

Spiritual Maturity, Spiritual Growth for reigning in the Kingdom of Heaven

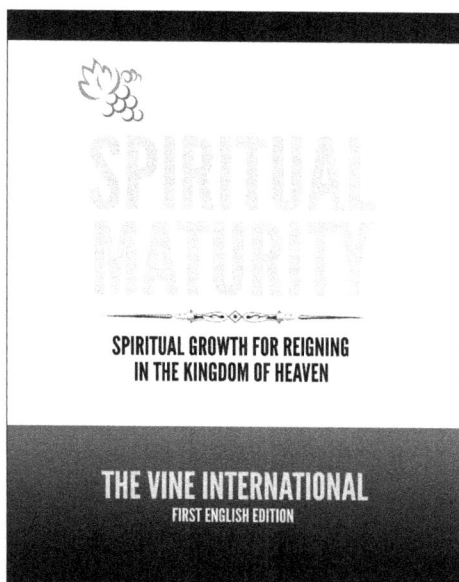

The purpose of this course is to form mature Christians instructed in the Word of God and able to minister to His people. In each chapter, we will be studying the most important biblical principles of the Christian life, such as walking in the Spirit, fleeing from sin and following the path of the overcomer. We will also study the safest ways to obtain spiritual revelation, how to be transformed in mind, will and emotions, how to have a renewed character and a full understanding of the Plan of Salvation. These are some of the issues dealt with in this course and are studied in the light of the basic premise of the New Testament that every Christian, including you, is destined to come to the full knowledge of the truth and serve as a minister in the spiritual house of God.

We believe that every lesson of this course will help you understand the Gospel and attain a mature and balanced Christian life. Therefore, we have divided this course into well-founded and objective lessons, which you will apply to your daily life and practice. At the end of each lesson, a list of questions has been included to help reinforce your understanding and retention of the content and principles presented through each lesson

Check out this book at:

http://www.amazon.com/Spiritual-Maturity-Course-Bundled-ebook/dp/B00BA2FOHG

Leadership training course, Effective leadership for small group ministry

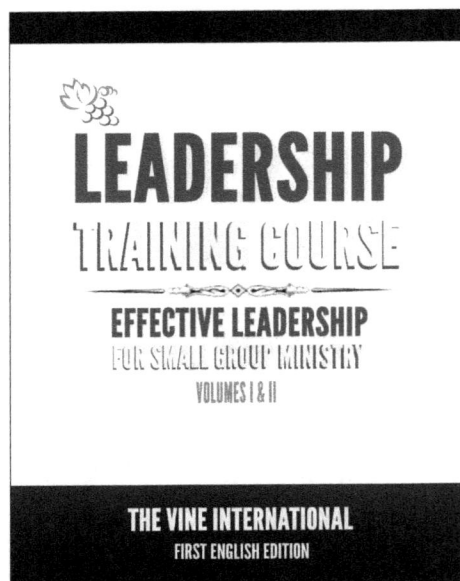

This course is an indispensable resource for small group leaders. God has called every Christian to fulfill the Great Commission. This implies that each Christian must develop leadership qualities by stepping up and developing his own quality leadership employing what he has learned by leading a small group. This leaders training course will help.

The leadership qualities of a small group leader are learned! Leaders are not born but cultivated, thus the need for a leaders training course. Jesus trained His own small group or "cell group" as we like to call them. These men began with no leadership qualities. They learned through the years they spent walking with Jesus. In the same way today, small group and cell group leaders must learn the principles that lead to effective leadership and these are not intuitively acquired. Quality leadership is always effective leadership. Leadership is about results and not just organization!

Each lesson of this resource shows how you as the leader of your cell group can identify and improve your leadership qualities and exercise an effective leadership resulting not only in your own growth, but also that of the members who you serve.

Christian leadership today is going through a tremendous crisis. The church has confused leadership with administration, which is important but not foundational! The small group leaders training course reinforces this distinction by teaching the proper identity we have as children of God and the purpose that God the Father has for each of His children. This course teaches the foundations of God's throne and how spiritual authority plays in extending His rule over the earth.

Each small group leader will learn effective leadership qualities by understanding and practicing these principles of spiritual authority. Spiritual authority has been woefully abused through the centuries and as a result many churches have abandoned the principle altogether. The Leadership training course shows how these principles can be practiced without getting lost in its abuses. It teaches the effective leadership qualities that new leaders need to protect themselves and the network of leaders in which they work from the dangers of these abuses.

Each small group leader will learn effective leadership qualities by observing the lives of OT and NT leaders like Moses, Joshua, David, and the Apostle Paul. The effective leadership qualities that these men practiced are often overlooked in the narrative of each gospel account. However, we must recognize that effective leadership qualities are the hallmark of each positive bible character and the negative characters in the bible are presented as models of leadership qualities that must be avoided.

Each small group leader will learn effective leadership qualities in evangelism, how to overcome barriers to evangelism, styles of evangelism, and tips for mobilizing your cell group in evangelism.

Each small group leader will learn effective leadership qualities related to praise and worship. Not every group member will have the gifts for ministering praise and worship but some will and you must know how to lead them into serving the group in this capacity.

Other things that this course will do for you:

- Increase your confidence as you grow in your conviction of your identity as a child and minister of God.
- Increase your competence for a more effective leadership in your small group.
- Increase your influence by growing in more effective leadership qualities. The focus is on effective leadership qualities and not just being recognized as a good friend or inspiring communicator.
- Increase your joy.
- Position you as a spiritual mother or father.

Check out this book at:

http://www.amazon.com/Leadership-Training-Course-Bundle-ebook/dp/B00BGUVWIW

Strengthening the New Christian, Consolidating new Believers

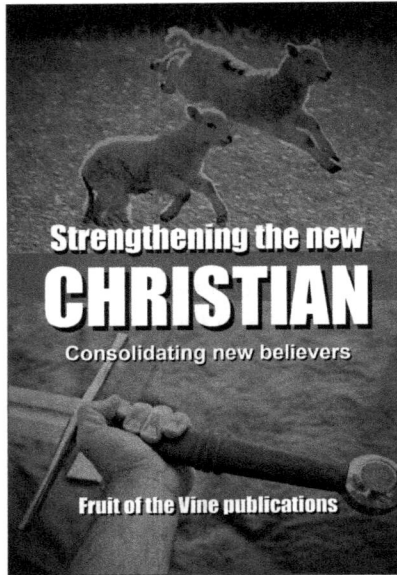

There are no ready-made formulas available for you to deal with each problem that may arise in your new life with Christ. However, when we are in the family, through discipleship and a close follow-up, we receive much more clarity about many things. In this manual, you will learn many things about the Word of God and about the New Birth, how to abandon the past and how to consecrate yourself. There are also lessons on how to forgive others, how to pray, among other indispensable disciplines that will strengthen you through your circumstances.

The lessons of this manual will help you better understand the importance of solid and long-lasting relationships since it is through this contact that you will be spiritually prepared to continue your new life in Christ. The purpose of this strengthening is to grow up into a mature disciple of Jesus able to reproduce in the lives of others that which has been wrought by God in you.

Check out this book at:

http://www.amazon.com/Strengthening-Christian-Consolidating-Believers-ebook/dp/B00AWT7YRG

The small group vision manual, how to fulfill the Great Commission through small groups

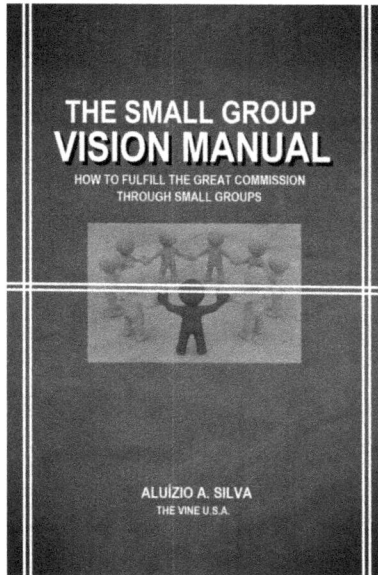

This manual was elaborated to help leaders with practical matters of organization, leadership and functioning of a cell group, besides helping them in each step along the way: strengthening, fellowship, evangelism, service and discipleship, in order to multiply one time each year. Throughout these pages we give a thorough explanation of our vision, why we are a church in cells, what a cell is and what its objectives are. In a simple but not superficial way, it's we also show who the key players in the cell are, their functions and how to deal with the members of the cell, besides discussing each part of the cell group meeting.

Here we illustrate our way of organizing ourselves and living as the church, but without a question, the enabling of the Holy Spirit is indispensable in order of for us to be able to multiply ourselves as the body of Christ. Our goal is not to convince anyone of the effectiveness of our work. Rather we invite you to dream with us! Dream about a generation that expresses the life of Christ through the family of God.

Check out this book at:

http://www.amazon.com/fulfill-Commission-through-Training-ebook/dp/B00BA08ND0

www.ingramcontent.com/pod-product-compliance
Lightning Source LLC
Chambersburg PA
CBHW072021060426
42449CB00033B/1355